Why Won't You Listen to Me!

Printed in the United States

ISBN: 1-58597-061-1

Library of Congress Catalog Control No. 00-134045

A division of Squire Publishers, Inc.
4500 College Blvd.
Leawood, KS 66211
1/888/888-7696

Why Won't You Listen to Me!

By

CHARLES R. JACKARD, Ed.D.

with

MICHAEL MCKENZIE

A division of Squire Publishers, Inc.
4500 College Blvd.
Leawood, KS 66211
1/888/888-7696

To my wife, Pat, whose faith, courage and love strengthen and guide me every day.

ACKNOWLEDGEMENTS

I am indeed grateful to the many students, parents and teachers who have so genuinely shared their challenges and celebrations with me. Those who have been crying out for help and have never been heard. Mixed with the experiences of their pain and frustrations, these people have taught me many things. In their struggles for survival they have become very wise. They join with me in the hope and prayer that others will begin to listen.

A special thanks to my children, Jane, Jeff and Jill, and my stepchildren, Cynthia and Greg. They have taught me to listen not only to words, but to the real meaning behind the words. To my sister, Anna, who has taught me the true meaning of unconditional love and acceptance.

Finally, to my grandchildren, Andrew, Hannah, Hayley and John. They have filled my life with joy and the assurance the best is yet to be.

FOREWORD

As I lay paralyzed in a hospital ward many years ago, feeling helpless and angry and afraid and confused by the swirling circumstances — a story you will read about in this book; indeed, a story that *inspired* this book — I made a conscious decision about how to spend the rest of my life.

I would walk again, contrary to the pessimism of doctors who would have tucked me away in a corner of an institution to babble and drool and depend on professional care givers. And when I could manage on my own, I would dedicate my every ounce of energy to helping three groups of people I had grown to love and care about — people I have been one of, and at one with.

I have dealt with all three groups in the dimmest hours of their frustrations, their discouragement, their despair over conditions of their lives, just like I experienced at times during my recovery. But I also have been among these people in times of joy and hope and optimism, when their sun was shining brightly through the dark clouds.

These people are parents and teachers and the youths in their charge.

Theirs is not an easy lot. But nobody promised it would be. Difficult or not, what I discovered in more than 20 years as an educator in a public school for troubled youths is that each parent, teacher, and student I ever dealt with was vulnerable in their humanness and looking for the good in life.

During those years as principal of the Alternative Education Program (AEP), a high school for young people with a wide variety of backgrounds and problems — things as simple as boredom with school and learning, and as complex as addiction and murder — I began to accumulate methods and research and personal experiences that would fill a book.

And so it has.

Over the last 35 years, I assimilated information and resources and turned them into classrooms and workshops for all persons who longed for insight into how to improve as a parent, a teacher, and a youth growing into adulthood.

At first, my wife, Pat (a solid rock in this and all projects I have undertaken, including getting well), and I participated in many forums for working in the field commonly known as At-Risk Education.

Then we staged our own national conference for a few years. Eventually, the wealth of resource material in my compendium of real-life in real-time — NOW — proved worthy of the formal classroom. Two needs fueled this avenue of reaching a critical mass: teachers constantly are required to stay abreast through continuing education, and teachers constantly are turning over every leaf in search of solutions to the mounting problems in dealing with problematic young people, K-through-12.

I designed numerous courses to address specific problem areas — personal communication skills, handling discipline, resolving conflict — implementing the methods that worked at the AEP, and that others shared from their similar environs. Several colleges and universities saw fit to include the courses in their curriculum for graduate credits.

That brings us up to the hour at hand. To supplement the courses, but also to reach an even wider base of persons seeking answers and rays of hope in troubled times, this book was born.

Through these pages you can gain insight and perspective from scores of individuals who have been there, done that on both sides of the fence — the offenders and the offended — and the parents and teachers and administrators and law enforcement officials and counselors who have ridden this emotional roller-coaster.

My own comeback story from extremely dire circumstances pales in comparison to many of the students you will hear about, and from (in their own words). Teachers often throw up their hands, feeling they are tied; well, imagine what the students who frustrate them feel like.

I mean that literally. At the heart of this work is a concept of empathy. The more compassion we can serve in the lives of troubled young people, the better choices they can make. It starts with understanding, and that leads off the book — how to strive for better understanding.

My strongest desire here is to establish an optimistic viewpoint and approach to what seems to many parents, teachers, and youths to be a dead-end, thus leading to burn-out, drop-out and, as one grim segment discusses, wipe-out.

Among the consciousness-raising material I have accumulated is a look at denial, the silent killer; unconditional love and acceptance in establishing authority and discipline (two things that often appear gone forever in the home and classroom and community); communication skills; coping techniques; a look at power and the issues it creates.

Interactive exercises — some individual, some group — help you measure and assess where you are, where you want to be, and how to get there. Use these tools. They are easy and they work.

Inspirational readings and affirmations accompany a wealth of research on empathy (with its own handy dictionary — the language of empathy), on the all-important topic of self-concept, and on components of communication (speaking, body language, listening). Special emphasis is placed on self-esteem and self-image as essential ingredients in successful interaction with other people, and it cuts both ways.

I also have included, as an appendix, an updated reworking of a booklet that Pat and I wrote long ago, *People Are People,* that holds timeless truths about how our common experiences as human beings can draw us together rather than split us apart.

You should enjoy the "T.L.C. Constitution," affirming the fundamental right to be loved ... the modern Four R's in education (respect, responsibility, right, and reality) that are as critical as the age-old three R's of reading, 'riting and 'rithmetic ... exercises on stereotyping, your care quotient, empathetic listening, and others.

Original poems speak of hope and despair and longing to belong. Histories gleaned from actual case files will stun you, not only in some of the behaviors taking place, but the wide variety of those behaviors. And almost every one moves toward violent resolution.

But as grim as some illustrations get, the message that I want to ring loud and clear is that each of us can do something about clearing away the grimness. Letters from parents, teachers, and students are rife with encouragement that these methods work.

Among the multitudes of teachers and administrators, staff, parents, and young persons I have encountered, I have found the vast majority to be well-intentioned.

But one of the first lessons of handling conflict is that the reason most people steer away from it is that they feel either incapable of dealing with the issues or they fear the consequences of dealing with the issues. Often, both.

Being assertive, though, simply means choosing to take action. Rolling up the sleeves and pant legs and wading in. Letting go of heavy-handed power and control, drawing upon compassion and understanding, and meeting the issues head-on ... with a smile, an extended hand, and love in your heart.

The greatest of these appears repeatedly as the crux of this work, for as one expert, Gerald Jampolsky, the founder of the Institute for Attitudinal Healing, put it as he learned it from The Course on Miracles:

Teach only love, for that is what you are.

CONTENTS

1

A Fighting Spirit: The Comeback Story

On July 7, 1985, with no previous symptoms or slightest hint of a problem, I awakened with no strength in my legs.

This was a shock to a staunch, active 49-year-old man of 6-feet-3, 215 pounds, who participated in athletics my entire life. I had been a scholarship basketball player and tennis player at Pittsburg State (Teachers College back then). I played tennis two hours a day even yet, at age 49. A friend, Bob Bates, and I ranked in the top five in doubles in the Missouri Valley Tennis Association during the first half of the '80s. I taught my three children to play well enough that they all earned college scholarships.

Now, suddenly, alarmingly, I could barely walk from my bed to my bathroom. And then, not at all.

I felt no pain. My legs looked normal. I was up early on a Sunday to meet Pat, who would become my wife in the near future (and whose strength and fighting spirit I drew from throughout a harrowing, long recovery period shrouded in mystery and misinformation).

The day before, my left arm had felt stiff, but I took

some medication and it felt fine this fateful morning. My legs, however, gave out. Completely. I could not move from my bathroom.

I dropped to my stomach and pulled myself across my apartment floor to the telephone. Literally, I covered inches at a time, wondering if I would make it as my strength waned and my mind registered alarm just short of panic.

Pat Jackard, nee Fornelli, answered my call, and she promptly dialed 911. She arrived at my side just ahead of the fire chief and three ambulances, and she had to break a window to enter because I had spent my last energy getting to the phone.

Ironically, paramedics thought I had experienced a drug overdose! The mystery began officially when my EKG registered normal, blood pressure registered normal and, fully conscious, I reported experiencing no pain whatsoever, chest, legs, anywhere. Yet, paralysis was setting in even as they tended to me.

Five hours of emergency surgery followed. The diagnosis came back: brain or spinal tumor, or blood vessels wrapped around the spine. Then it changed: multiple sclerosis. And it changed again before that first traumatic night ended: Guillan-Barre Syndrome.

I had never heard of it. Now, I can give you an enlightened discourse on this rare condition that behaves like a virus. Sort of like an acid, the syndrome destroys nerve-conducting tissue and disrupts the communication between brain and muscles. The syndrome renders the legs, arms, and sometimes facial muscles useless.

One memorable major headline garnered by Guillan-

Barre syndrome over the years was when several cases developed among persons after they had swine flu shots. Another time, famed actor Andy Griffith was felled by the syndrome. Author Joseph Heller *(Catch-22)* had it, too, and wrote a book about the experience, *No Laughing Matter.*

About one-fourth of the time, victims experience total paralysis and the respiratory system shuts down, sometimes fatally. Otherwise, the prognosis is optimistic — slow, but full recovery. Pat Fornelli Jackard looks back in her diary notes of three days after the attack on me and finds, "… Illness will be a long haul, 1-2 years recovery. Can't be true. Pray, Pat, pray."

* * * * * * * * * *

Pat Fornelli and I met in 1976 when she worked at Shawnee Mission (Kan.) Alternative Education Program, where I was director and principal. Pat has been executive director of the nationally acclaimed Singles Ministry at Village Presbyterian Church in Prairie Village, Kan., since 1985. We married in November 1986.

A story about me in *The Kansas City Star Magazine* (Sept. 7, 1986) said: "Pat calls Charles 'a very rigid German.' He jokes about her Italian flair for drama. Charles speaks with very little emotion …

[… that would come as a shock to the hundreds of teachers and parents who have listened to me at school, in my lectures, and during my continuing education or national workshops, as my emotions rise in earnest over my

passion for enhancing the lives of challenged, at-risk young people ....]

... whether discussing his beloved tennis game or his physical condition and challenges."

Before the Guillan-Barre attack, I was planning with Pat for a national series of seminars they wanted to create from a book we wrote together in 1983, *Commandments for Communicating, Coping and Controlling,* and from my earlier work, *People are People* . Those plans went on hold.

The happy ending to this story is that eventually we staged the national conference for educators of students at risk and made numerous appearances on demand for our insight and models at other national gatherings of educators. But it was a long, often discouraging, journey through wheelchairs, canes, no voice, mixed medical reports, anger and agonizing rehabilitation to reach that point.

Confused, feeling helpless and sometimes hopeless, I faltered at times.

* * * * * * * * * * * *

From Pat's diary, July 16, 1985: "Worst day ever. Charles' veins have totally shut down. He's given up. I can't believe it. He tells me, 'Honey, I may have to go on a respirator.' Be brave."

Rarely have victims of Guillain-Barre died, at least not since the early years of its discovery around 1900, but many have suffered respiratory failure. The lungs simply shut down. I underwent a procedure called plasma pheresis eight times. It is very painful. It did no good whatsoever for me. A tracheotomy was next, giving me breath but stealing my voice.

Pat noted in her diary that I looked "really, really bad … there is something very, very wrong," after a bout with pneumonia. Doctors told her that my life was hanging in the balance, that I might not make it through the night (July 19, just 12 days after the attack), that she should call my family in for a final visitation. Eventually, they would suggest that three times.

She wrote, "He will make it, I'm sure. God can't be done with this man yet."

Certainly we know that now. I knew nothing at the time. I couldn't conceive that I was that sick. Believe it, I was — with a tube down my throat, my lungs hooked to a machine, and unable to motion or speak. I spent three months in intensive care, virtually helpless, with a towel draped across my waist.

Looking back, that was the most frustrating time of my life. I was aware of everything going on around me, but I couldn't talk or even respond to anything. When I hurt, I couldn't tell anybody. Pat would recite the alphabet, and I would blink on a letter until I spelled out the words I wanted to say. It took forever for us to get a few words out.

I also learned the deepest meaning of the word humiliation; I had no bladder or bowel control. And I lay motionless as I witnessed — almost like an out-of-body experience, my mind fully alert while my huge frame was rendered still — when nurses carried out "Code Blue" procedures to keep my lungs cleared of congestion.

You get the picture. It wasn't pretty, and there were no clear reasons for me to believe that it would ever get pretty again. My tennis partner and friend, Bob Bates, told the magazine writer, "Charlie was physically strong (and) mentally agile — a tough competitor … it was amazing to see him reduced to a shell. It was like felling a redwood. He was a rock."

In mid-September of '85 I moved to a rehab hospital unit. Depression set in. I became, by all accounts (including my own) obstinate, grouchy and more stubborn than ever. I felt dehumanized, and my sermonizing on that topic intensifies greatly because of the treatment I received and subsequent feelings during recovery.

In yet another twist of irony, as a man dedicated to helping others, I declined help from others. I refused psychiatric counseling. I snapped at persons attempting to assist me. My physical therapist, Bob Meredith, said that he couldn't believe that friends were talking about the same guy ("witty, sense of humor") that he was dealing with.

"That was his biggest challenge," Pat says. "He had never had to focus his attention inward. I didn't mind him being cantankerous, because to me that was a sign that his spirit was still strong, somewhere deep inside. I just wanted everyone to know what a truly neat, wonderful person he was."

This, the guy who spat his oatmeal back at her when she tried to feed him? The guy who sarcastically put down her posting of a get-well-soon sign? Yes, him …

me, the man she would marry (maybe the biggest miracle of all!).

Over time, I began to draw on my teaching materials, especially a technique known as imaging, or visualization. I started acting on the key buzzwords in our books — accepting, coping, controlling. I made the transition from a "Why me?" victim to a proactive rehabilitation process.

And I made a conscious commitment and vow that has guided me to this point, and to whatever lies beyond: "I will use this experience in a positive realm."

Self-respect was the first rung of the ladder that I urged my at-risk students at school to climb to higher ideals and achievements. I knew that I had to build on that same concept. As I wrote in *People Are People,* "It is a marvelous thing to learn from despair."

I heard from hundreds of my former students when I couldn't rejoin them for the 1985 school year. I left the hospital about the time they were adjourning for the summer, May of '86. I was a shell of my former self, down 45 pounds, shuffling slowly with assistance of a cane when I was out of a wheelchair.

I dived into my rehab with the grit of my former tennis-playing days. Fifteen years later, I have full use of all muscles, and no lingering effects of Guillain-Barre. No physical effects, that is.

But I sustain the lingering and career-driving effect of personal struggle on the mental side. Doctors said when I left the hospital that persons with less determination give in to the syndrome, sometimes even die. At the core of all of my teaching and preaching lies one constant, central premise:

You cannot always control what happens to you, but you can always control how you respond to what happens to you ...and there always is hope for something good to happen.

2

Case Histories

During 20 years at a high school that included drop-outs and dope dealers, pregnants and punks, jailbirds and junkies, the case studies of various miscreants formed a mountain, not a molehill, in the principal's office. Remember, I wasn't in an inner city, ghetto environment. This school provided an alternative to one of the most affluent school districts in the United States, one that has been held up as a model of excellence in scholastic achievement in the suburbs of Kansas City.

The cases presented here demonstrate the variety of problematic behaviors across the spectrum of the dark side of suburbia and school. The tales illustrate how inventive the students are at pulling scams, how overt they are in violent behavior and damn the consequences, and how impressionable they are from home life.

Because of space constraints, I omitted several stories: a kid stealing $170 from his mother and saying it was for car insurance when it was for drugs ... three girls threatening to beat another because she refused to pay up an $8.50 phone bill charged to one of the girls' phone

… a former student banned from the school grounds because after showing up to deliver flowers to a girl who had broken up with him for abusing her, he followed her around, called her names, and harassed her ceaselessly … a student trading a book for a compact disc; the book, "The Mischievous Cook Book," was taken off of the Internet, he said, and it contained several "recipes" for making bombs and other explosive devices.

The case histories involved knives and various guns (hand guns, shotgun, pellet gun) … about three-fourths of the cases involved fighting and threats of violence and bodily harm … about the same percentage of students in the case histories, all minors, had been in trouble with the law … thievery was rampant.

The stories come straight from the reports of the school's Police Resource Officer (PRO), assigned by the county sheriff's office in case of emergency situations, sometimes in uniform, sometimes in plain clothes, mostly out of sight in the front office.

Names are changed, and some editorial license helps the storytelling. But nothing is exaggerated. These are real kids. These things happened. Oh, did they ever happen.

They continue to happen, and that is the sad side of this segment. The glad side is that, perhaps, with renewed insight and enthusiasm on our part as educators, as parents, and as concerned citizens, we can stem the tide. Virtually all the young people I dealt with in the alternative environment wanted just one thing – a chance to do good.

They were looking for people to guide them, not to look down their noses at them; to show them a better way, to demonstrate some hopefulness and encouragement. Not a lot to ask, when you think about it.

* * * * * * * * * *

Buddy sauntered up to Sapphire in the hallway. He nudged her, and she gave him a hook-look, that "get outta my face" glare, and she muttered something. He didn't catch what she said, but there was no mistaking the way she said it.

He couldn't take that, not if he was to be a man. That's what his father taught him, he said later. "Not to take squat off anybody, especially not no girl." That's why he had told Dawn just a few days earlier how he'd knock the hell out of her if she gave him any guff. So she didn't. She didn't even report him for threatening her.

Now, here was Sapphire, acting like she was all that when Buddy touched her. He'd touch her, all right. Bitch. "You know," Buddy said to her, within earshot of several students in the hallway, "I could bring a gun to school and put it to your head."

He grinned. Sapphire didn't. And another student who heard it, a friend of Dawn's who had heard the remarks to her, too, didn't find it funny, either. One of the unwritten rules of the school was an honor code, geared to self-policing. Instead of expensive surveillance equipment in every nook and cranny ("Big Brother is watching"), and a cadre of uniformed police wandering the hallways, the students set the standards for unacceptable behavior.

And a threat of bodily harm, especially the threat of firearms, was a definite no-no. As it turned out, more than one student who heard Buddy reported him. When confronted, he admitted what he had said to both girls.

Criminal charges were filed against him through the District Attorney's office. Buddy was expelled from school. He avoided jail by the skin of his teeth, but was placed on strict probation and house arrest that severely restricted his freedom.

All the stories don't have happy endings. But they all have a moral. Or two.

* * * * * * * * * * *

Raoul pushed the envelope too hard, and he's going down.

It started with a phone call from Missy, who wanted a ride. She wasn't a student at AEP, like him. She was younger, in middle school. He didn't care. A score's a score. He knew she got around, even if she couldn't drive yet.

Raoul picked Missy up at her house. He didn't go to the door. He knew that her mother didn't like him, and this being Easter Sunday and all. They drove around, exchanged idle talk. About school being a drag, he told police. About parents being a drag, she told police.

You know, teenage stuff. At some point, Raoul flashed weed. Awright. She smoked it with him. But she couldn't handle it. As they walked back to his car, she fell, landing hard on concrete and cutting her head. Raoul didn't panic, but he also didn't take her for medical assistance. He immediately drove her back home, and sped away quickly after she got out.

Missy's mother called the school on Monday and reported Raoul for getting her daughter high, leading to an injury. He already had a possession charge at AEP hanging over his head in probationary status. An investigation turned up evidence that he had been hanging out at one of the district high schools, moving weed.

Raoul was charged with endangerment of a child, and his case was turned over to the DA's office for prosecution. He became one of the stream of students who wrote me a letter of regret and remorse.

From jail.

* * * * * * * * * * *

Mike came to the PRO scared. He wasn't afraid of Darrel, who was threatening him. At least that's what Mike's girlfriend, Chris, said. Chris used to be Darrel's girl, and he told her that he was hiring Matt to shoot Mike.

Not only was Darrel out of sorts over losing his girlfriend, but he also suspected that Mike was somehow involved in the shooting of Darrel's close friend Jeremy, who died. Soap operas like this played out all the time at AEP.

Mike told the school policeman what his real fear was: "I don't want to have to take my gun to prom to protect myself." He was afraid that Darrel or his henchman, Matt, or both would show up at the prom as guests of somebody, with the sole intent of taking him down.

Because Mike was forthcoming with this information, effective intervention took place. School officials called in both Darrel and Matt and informed them that their conspiracy was known. They didn't bother Mike or Chris again.

And Mike, after learning of the consequences if he carried a gun to the prom, did not carry at the dance. He said that it had been hard for him to inform the school of the goings-on, rather than just handling it in silence, his way, violently if necessary.

He actually thanked the people involved at the school for their help. "At first I didn't trust (the system) if I ratted out," he told the PRO cop. "I figured it would just make it worse. But it helped me to understand that I have to take responsibility for my actions."

* * * * * * * * * *

Jeremy, not the same Jeremy who was shot to death, and a former AEP student, Chuck, lied about the attempted robbery of a bank ATM, in broad daylight — 2 o'clock — in a crowded mall.

This wasn't a stick-'em-up robbery, so they figured it was too slick an operation for them to get caught. Who was going to know they were using somebody else's credit card to withdraw from the ATM?

They didn't know about the surveillance camera. Jeremy's face was on it, clear as day. That's how AEP got the call; local police said they suspected one of the AEP students and a former student were among the three persons in the robbery.

The credit cards they used in the theft had been stolen in a reported auto burglary in the mall parking lot just 10 minutes before the boys hit the bank ATM for cash flow.

* * * * * * * * * * *

"I'm going to kick your ass!" Jason shouted in front of maybe 20 other students, threatening Ralph. Now that might not seem like such a radical report from an intervention officer — maybe just another schoolyard fight, or threat of one.

Trouble was, Ralph was driving the school bus that the other 20 kids were riding on along with Jason. When confronted, Jason was contrite as the officer explained to him that not only was a violent act unlawful, but even the public threat of one was unlawful.

"I know it was wrong," Jason said. "But you don't understand. I hate Ralph. If I had a chance, I'd pound his head into the side of the bus and then run over him with the bus."

He said that Ralph never had done anything to him to warrant such feelings. It was just a general dislike. He thought Ralph was nerdy, and too bossy with students about being quiet on the bus. Jason's logic, as we learned, was the logic in his house when somebody lipped off or otherwise seemed out of line for whatever reason, small or large, was that an ass-whipping was deserved.

He was all the more incensed that Ralph had the nerve to write him up on the bus for the threatening behavior. When Jason was prohibited from riding the bus any more during the school year, he left the police officer with a clear impression that he didn't get it.

What do you think? Jason's departing words were, "I can always get somebody else to handle Ralph and give me an alibi."

* * * * * * * * * * *

Sapphire, revisited. Johnny and James were the other players this time. And the deal wasn't threats of violence, it was drugs. Not just any drugs, but LSD.

The threesome was caught because tension and loud words were spoken during the transaction. Who would have heard such a shady, clandestine deal for acid? Surely it was in some back alley, or in a dark corner of the mall parking lot, or, well, what other stereotypes do you have in mind?

The heated exchange was heard by many because it took place in the school hallway. It was heated because Sapphire was trying to stiff the dealer, James. He had fronted her eight hits of acid, and she agreed to pay him $40 later. When later came, Sapphire didn't have the $40.

Enter Johnnie. He conspired with her to tell James that she gave him the money to give to James, whom he didn't know, and that he gave it to the wrong person, somebody he also hadn't seen before and couldn't identify.

After the two students were reported to the office and interviewed, they admitted to the concocted scheme and were put on probation. But they also helped bring down a street dealer; Sapphire reported that James gave her the LSD from a sheet of about 70-80 hits that he bragged about dealing. Police tracked him, caught him supplying, and put him out of business ... at least temporarily.

* * * * * * * * * * *

Miss Hathaway's class was about to convene. But just

before the bell, all fury broke loose.

Olivia charged up to her classmate Keisha, screaming epithets at her and flailing away with punches. When Miss Hathaway stepped in to separate the two (Keisha was not retaliating; she was ducking and covering her face and head with her arms), Olivia knocked her down.

"You whore!" Olivia screamed, pounding on Keisha. That was the tip-off to what was at the center of this outburst. Boy trouble.

"I was with her cousin over the weekend," Keisha explained, "and got caught by his pregnant girlfriend."

Cousin George's girlfriend was Olivia's best friend, but, typically, instead of confronting George for his promiscuity, Olivia waited to take revenge on Keisha. That twisted thinking bought Olivia a five-day suspension from school and probationary status for the rest of the school year.

Keisha, feeling sympathetic — "I probably would be upset, too" – did not press criminal assault charges, but said she would be on the alert and report any further retaliation. The school year passed without any further incidents between them.

* * * * * * * * * *

Mike, a known drug user, suspected addict: "What happens if I bring a gun to school?"

Teacher: "You'd be immediately kicked out of school, suspended, perhaps permanently, and probably arrested."

Mike: "I wasn't seriously thinking about it. I was kidding. I just wondered."

Surveillance was established on Mike, in case he thought he had cleverly diverted attention. He never packed.

But a week later he wound up in lock-up anyway. His father called and said that Mike was incarcerated at the juvenile detention center for disorderly conduct. He got involved in a fracas the night before, and afterward informed his father and authorities that he had taken drugs at school during the day.

His father was distraught and bewildered about what steps to take. He said that when he arrived at the police station Mike was belligerent and out of control. "He kept saying that he has no family, that the gang is his family," Mike's father told the school officials.

He said that Mike had failed a drug screening, and that he had stole some of his mother's medication and sold it to friends at school. The PRO report said, "This is possibly a good explanation of what happened Thursday when other students displayed the same type behavior as Mike."

Mike's parents requested that he remain locked up and receive intervention counseling for his drug problem. Authorities granted their request and detained him for at least one month, to be followed by evaluation.

In a conversation with school officials, Mike's mother said that he admitted to taking Xanax from her medicine supply to school, and told her of other activity going on there — mostly marijuana distribution and smoking pot in the bathrooms — and she named six other boys.

A few days later, some of the boys Mike had named to her were overheard talking on two occasions about marijuana smoking sessions. One of them, Mark, told a fellow student, "That stuff got me so high I couldn't walk home straight. I ended up walking into the wrong house."

Later that day, a student at school for his first day, also named Mike, seemed unusually popular. A crowd was around him at various times during the day. When a student named Brian said too loud, "Put me down for some," a teacher moved in and found the new kid on the block writing down orders.

The new Mike lasted a week. A student reported attending a party at another student's house, staged while his father was in the hospital. At the party, new-Mike's father was providing liquor to kids there, mostly minors (the legal drinking age in Kansas was 18, for beer only).

Turns out that the parent in the hospital didn't live at the house anyway; he stayed with relatives to receive medical care. His son, Matthew, lived there with a roommate, and they had a thriving marijuana business.

Lo and behold, new Mike was soon caught and charged with possession and dealing. Subtlety was not his strong suit.

* * * * * * * * * *

From a PRO report: "I received a call from a former student, Jake, who said he overheard at a party that three or four subjects were coming to AEP next week to engage in a gun fight with two students. This is supposed to take place during the last smoke break, and the subjects will be walking on foot from the area of the (nearby) driver's license bureau and across the ball fields.

"The students are supposed to be aware of this, and are supposed to be armed. No other identification could be obtained from Jake on either group. I suggest that the city P.D. (police) be advised, and I will advise members of the sheriff's gang unit."

* * * * * * * * * *

The case load goes on and on and on. One of a teenager sexually involved with his younger sister. A 28-year-old woman taking liberties with a minor, who in turn was taking liberties with her young daughter. Love triangles galore. Revenge. Drug deals and deals gone bad, involving marijuana, LSD, cocaine, and crystal meth.

And you thought *Blackboard Jungle*, circa 1959 (book by Evan Hunter, movie with Glenn Ford), was fiction. And only in the Bronx.

We'll end with this drama, on the theme of it's hard to fight the enemy even when you know who — or in these case studies, what — it is, but all the harder when you don't even know. And that is so symbolic of what's happening with all of these kids, out there perceiving you and me and dad and mom and the boogie man as the enemy, caught in a survival of the fittest game, and struggling day to day to survive it.

God help them. God help us help them.

* * * * * * * * * *

Jan. 19. Chris and her counselor, Ms. Dodderidge, met with the AEP counselor and police officer. Chris was upset no end. She had learned that her boyfriend was involved in a situation a year earlier, admitting to his participation in a shooting in which a youth was murdered.

The only specifics she revealed was that somebody had been convicted of the murder. Her problem now was that her boyfriend had told other friends about this, and the story was spreading. She feared repercussions.

A cousin to the victim in the shooting attends school with her at AEP, another girl. Chris was afraid, trembling visibly, but stubbornly refused intervention from the school officials or the law. She decided to go discuss it further with her boyfriend.

Feb. 15 Two men arrived on the AEP campus today, asking for Chris. They said they were there to pick her up from school.

She had not filed for an early dismissal.

As the men stood in the office, Chris walked by. The men looked right at her, but did not show any sign of recognition. They clearly did not know who they were after. Later, Chris revealed that she did not recognize either man, judged to be in their 30s and driving a van with an Ohio license plate.

Nothing ever showed up in the files again on this case. Chris graduated from AEP.

The haunting, seemingly bleak unknown future for Chris, and thousands like her, provides strong motivation for involvement with troubled youths.

We must press on.

Felt I Was Too Old

I felt I was too old.
Cocaine stole my father,
Work took my mother,
I felt responsible for my sisters,
'Cause I was their older brother.
For Mom, by herself, the bills were too much,
Overwhelmed, and now homeless,
used alcohol as her crutch.
For me, I was alone, scared and sad.
I wanted to cry but couldn't 'cause crying was weak,
and weakness was bad.
I hated poverty and all the feelings it bared,
So I yelled to the world, but they didn't listen,
turned their back, never cared.
This made me mad at the world,
I wondered why they responded to my yells with silence.
So I learned to get what I wanted, not by asking,
but taking their violence.
Money meant everything to me; life, it meant none.
Peace, it only stayed in my dreams. My reality was a gun.
Now at 16, sitting in jail, I realize childhood is gold.
But now, it's too late 'cause at 11, I felt I was too old.

—John Cornett, a student

3

The 4 Critical R's

Traditionally, the fundamental core of education has been the teaching of the three R's – readin', 'ritin', and 'rithmetic.

In today's world of rising drug use, violence, teen pregnancy, teen suicide, and assorted other disruptions of the education system, the time has arrived for revising the basic approach to the fundamentals of learning to revolve around ***FOUR*** R's, and avoiding some ineffective P's that get in the way.

The four critical R's:

- Respect
- Responsibility
- Right (from wrong)
- Reality

The P's creating the stumbling blocks:

- Power
- Punishment
- Prison

Much too often we find school boards, administrators, and teachers overtly resorting to power plays, controlling tactics, and punishment as the first and strongest responses to students whose attitude and behavior is to "upt" the education system and process (interrupt, disrupt, corrupt).

This role power approach simply does not work. Until we earn the respect of each student and provide a base of unconditional acceptance and love, underscored with discipline and empathy, we cannot expect changes in behavior and results. (On the matter of discipline, remember one of the steps is establishing right from wrong. You will find that this approach is not about a touchy-feely, soft, kid-gloves treatment; it absolutely supports strong, assertive, demanding, and consequential standards to be met.)

As the adage goes, keep doing what you're doing and you'll keep getting what you're getting.

A revolution is in order. Sympathy, understanding, and acceptance lie at the heart of the revolution.

I have had the privilege, and severe challenge, of working with thousands of lost and aimless youths over the last 30 years, in both urban and suburban environs. Most have grown listless and hopeless, turning to irresponsible behaviors, with drugs and violence at the outermost extreme.

My experience indicates that when these youngsters interact with persons who love them unconditionally, yet love them enough to provide necessary discipline and guidelines, they respond favorably. Not in every single, solitary case, of course. But the failures were a result of their own bad choices when they could have made good ones, NOT a breakdown in the methodology.

These guiding principles have reached a far higher percentage of the so-called at-risk students and led to more positive results than those based on forms of punishment as a primary motivator for changing undesirable behavior. In actuality, threats of punishment (which usually lead to banishment, and then the student is washed out of the system entirely) prove to be poor deterrents, according to study after study that show drastic change in the wrong direction; i.e., rising drug use, crime, violent acts (including suicide), AIDs, and teen pregnancy all increased during the 1990s.

The greatest gifts we can give our youth is to accept them and believe in them.

* * * * * * * * * *

With fear and punishment as primary applications intended to alleviate problems among wayward youths, take a look at some results:

- A federally-sponsored survey revealed that drug use among teenagers more than doubled since 1992.

- A National Household Survey conducted annually by the Department of Health and Human Services showed in 1995 that 10.9 percent of respondents 12-17 years old used illicit drugs during the month before the survey. That was up 105 percent from 5.3 percent in 1992.

- The same survey measured use of marijuana up 141

percent and use of LSD and other hallucinogens up 183 percent in a three-year period. Cocaine use rose 166 percent in ONE year, between the 1994 and 1995 surveys.

- The Center for Health and the National Center for Disease Control and Prevention conducted a joint study in 1996 and found similar alarming increases in teenagers smoking pot, and an alarming increase in suicide by teenagers despite an increase in education and prevention programs.

Wherein lies the blame?

Well, to paraphrase from the ancient Tao in Asian philosophy: The ignorant only cast blame; wise people seek solutions.

All of us can spin ourselves into butter attempting to pinpoint where the fault lies. Rather, let's join hands and spend that energy on finding ways to meet the challenge of reversing the dismal trends.

The first step is recognition of the problem, not turning a blind eye. Many people generalize by blasting parents and society as a whole. The point is, many young people bring major problems to school, and you and I must strengthen our commitment – individually, and collectively – to do everything within our power to assist them in overcoming. The easiest thing to do is shrug, give up, and cast blame.

Another pothole, besides denial or generalized labeling and finger-pointing, is being PC. It is politically correct, for example, to allocate funds for prisons and a system for incarcerating youthful offenders. Some observers say that more is spent that way than in building schools and paying teachers.

It looks good on the discipline record to kick 'em out and lock 'em up. Zero tolerance programs are popping up all over the educational system. Please understand clearly that in 25 years as a principal and director of an alternative education high school, in which we had every shape and form of offender and problem child, we drew clear lines on what behavior was acceptable and unacceptable. And the students understood clearly what the consequences of their choices would be.

This is not a plea for going soft, for pampering, or for tolerating totally unacceptable or irresponsible acts. Rather, this is a plea for filtering compassion, understanding and acceptance into whatever standards of discipline and responsible action is required.

Let's review the Four R's:

RESPECT: Until you earn the student's respect by respecting the student, changed patterns cannot be expected. Teaching them respect for self, for each other, for you, and for their opportunities leads to an increase in learning academically, plus the youngsters will acquire the necessary skills to survive in and contribute productively to their community.

RESPONSIBILITY: For a more clear working definition, break up the word this way – response-ability. Help the students foster their ability to respond to situations and choices in positive ways, with positive outcomes. The main thrust is to teach the individual to take full responsibility for his or her own results.

RIGHT (vs. Wrong): Troubled young people must know precisely what is acceptable to allow them to move forward with their lives, and the just rewards for doing the right thing. Conversely, they must have a clearly understood knowledge of the consequences if they continue to choose to violate policy, infringe on others' rights, and disrupt the education process.

REALITY: In schools and families we have to face what is going on and get our heads out of the sand, stop acting like the problems don't exist. Problems don't make the school bad; what's bad is when the schools don't acknowledge the reality of what is occurring with our young people. How many lost souls do we have to lose? Or worse, how many lives before we hear them crying out for help, right under our noses, in suburbia as well as the depressed city areas, and across all social lines.

* * * * * * * * * *

I promise you, from years of experience and thousands of case results, these directives work. The kids are crying out for this kind of treatment and direction.

Give it to them. Start with a fifth R:

Right now.

Teaching with Compassion, Not Power

If I do not want what you want, please try not to tell me that my want is wrong.

Or, if I believe other than you, at least pause before you correct my view.

Or, if my emotion is less than yours, or more, given the same circumstances, try not to ask me to feel more strongly or more weakly.

Or, yet if I act, or fail to act, in a manner of your design for action, let me be.

I do not, for the moment at least, ask you to understand me. ***That will come only when you are willing to give up changing me into a copy of you.***

I may be your student, your offspring, your sibling, your friend, your peer. If you will allow me any of my own wants, or emotions, or beliefs, or actions, then you open yourself, *so that some day these ways of mine might not seem so wrong, and might finally appear to you as right —**for me!***

To put up with me is the first step to understanding me.

Not that you embrace my ways as right for you, but that you are no longer irritated or disappointed with me for my seeming waywardness. And in understanding me, you might come to prize my differences from you, and, far from seeking to change me, preserve and even nurture those differences.

— From *Please Understand Me*
by David Keirsey and Marilyn Bates

* * * * * * * * * *

Educators, arise. Mount a steed of optimism; throw off the shackles of discouragement, frustration and burnout. Push forward with renewed energy and commitment. America's youth, America's future, is counting on you.

Your student is crying out, and the message is clear: s/he thinks nobody understands, nobody cares ... nobody's there.

We *can* understand. We *must* understand. And care, and be there.

Or pay a terrible price in lost hope, and lost youth.

A preponderance of evidence continues to mount that shows an alarming percentage of today's youth heading down dead-end paths. I contend that a big reason is that our method of dealing with the problem also takes a dead-end approach.

Such an indictment might seem harsh, for without question a vast majority of professional educators have excellent intentions. But the teacher burnout rate seems directly proportionate to the student dropout rate, and alternative education programs and juvenile detention centers are bulging at the walls.

Another large reason for the gloomy side of the big picture is that all too often parents and educators alike operate with our heads in the sand. Pot, cocaine, PCP, heroin, hand guns and other weapons? Why, those things go down on the dark side of the inner city, right? Surely not in our affluent neighborhoods, not in suburbia.

Tell that to Englewood, Colo., home of Columbine High. Tell that to Plano, Tex., where several teenagers died last year from overdoses of heroin.

The problems are everywhere, pervasive in all segments of our society, every profile.

I believe so strongly that denial is the most deadly silent killer. Denial comes not only from not wanting to believe that these dreadful behaviors run rampant through all of our children's school and peer groups, but also from concern of the powers-that-be over the image of their schools and communities.

Today, high test scores, academic achievement, and progressive classrooms are prominent themes, and the political pressure is great on teachers to foster the image. Therefore, the scope of underlying problems is downplayed.

Finally, in the mainstream of education, educators struggle against difficult odds (lack of funding, overpopulated classrooms, etc.) and feel embattled, exhausted from day-to-day survival, so a notion grows that it's a lost cause. A prevailing attitude of "what can I, just one person, do?" saturates the profession.

In these pages you will read some horror stories. Many of them have happy endings, or at least rays of hope and optimism lighting the path to good possibilities.

Once we acknowledge that the problems exist and commit with unwavering determination to confront them, the starting point is understanding — an empathetic approach to education, rather than a power play. *Understand the problem as it exists; then understand the student, as s/he reaches out for guidance and better choices and the ingredient lacking most — love and acceptance.*

Without abandoning time-honored tradition and basics, we can instill trust, faith, and hopefulness in our youth while still striving for the best test scores, college admittance rates, and all the other things that boards of education and superintendents love because they keep parents off their back and tax dollars flowing.

Let's dig in and find out how we can have the best of both worlds, and cling joyfully to the noble mission of teaching that drove us into the classroom in the first place.

5

The Power of Empathy

Empathy is defined by one source as projecting your own personality into the personality of someone else in order to understand that person better; the ability to share in another person's emotions and feelings. (Daniel Lionel, 1990). We commonly call it relating. *(See definitions, Appendix I.)*

Skillful application of empathy stretches the potential to impact positively on all personal and professional relationships. Problems of drug addiction, abusive relationships, crime, even war would likely decrease if people increased their dosages of empathy.

We all benefit from understanding, and being understood. One researcher (Bernice Weissbourd, 1996) demonstrated the importance of parents and family members to show empathy for young children. The basic need for nurturing must be met in the formative years to create a healthy basis for human development. The lack of affection from parents links directly to an adult's fear of intimacy.

All relationships are enhanced by empathy. Teachers

must empathize with students to create the best conditions for learning that meets the student's needs. Students, in turn, can empathize with teachers when they fall behind in grading papers or fall ill.

A consumer is more likely to buy from a sales clerk who expresses understanding. Co-workers get along better when they express understanding of everyone's unique style in thinking and performing tasks. Empathy in any setting, any relationship, makes room for creativity and diminishes conflict and criticism.

Conversely, the absence of empathy leads to negative results. Highly dysfunctional families. Dissolved marriages and friendships. Declining profit and instability in business. Rising rates of violence and addiction.

Empathy spread among people in all environments makes the difference between depression and joy in everyday life.

Empathy could be the strongest get-well treatment in society.

Writings on Empathy

In my curriculum in a social studies class, I require students to create a poetry collection and write essays on a theme. These are samples of a student's works on the theme of empathy. Dee Herdman said she chose the theme after studying and meditating on the idea of how empathy could change lives dramatically in many settings, alter and strengthen primary relationships, and ultimately change the world we live in for the better.

"My Face, Your Face"

My face is not like your face,
But
I know how it feels to
laugh, to cry,
to belong, to be left out,
to have pride.

My face is not the same as your face,
yet,
I feel bad when you
look the other way,
avoid me,
withdraw.

I am not you,
but
I care when you feel bad.
I understand because
I have troubles, too.

My face and yours are different,
but
if you need somebody to listen,
to understand just how it is...
just tell me what you are feeling,
and you'll see on my face that I care.

"Empathy"

Emerging
Meaningful
Personal
Affirming
Trust-building
Helpfulness
YES!!

"How Empathy Could Change the World"

If King Empathy ruled the world,
There would be no war,
No poor,
If Empathy could reign
There would be much less grief,
Much less pain.

If people listened to the needs of others
And then consulted Empathy,
Citizens of the world would
Meet each other's needs
As well as have their own needs
Attended to
Without asking.

O, hear me, gracious King Empathy,
Spread your wisdom through this land.
Help us join together, hand in hand.
Take your teachings from shore to shore
Until unity and harmony grew to be more
On people's hearts and on their minds.

Bring all together, teach us to be kind.
Disputes and differences aside,
Let us in peace now abide.

Hand in hand, one and all,
We thank you, Lord Empathy,
For hearing our humble call.

* * * * * * * * * *

Ms. Herdman also wrote an autobiographical sketch of her childhood that demonstrated a lack of empathy; a review of the movie "Searching for Bobby Fischer" with examples of how the star, a young boy, demonstrated empathy on all fronts; and she concluded her assignments with an excerpt from her personal journal (edited for space considerations):

I play many roles: woman, daughter, girlfriend, teacher, friend, student, employee.

As a woman I understand issues such as feminine stereotypes, health matters, gender roles.

As a daughter, I know what it means to grow from a girl to a women under the rules of a disjointed family ... to be the older sister...to be 7 and devastated...to have four parents who care.

As a girlfriend, I know what it means to have a companion who cares for and adores me...to have a special person to love, to miss, to help, to enjoy.

As a friend, I know what it means to join together for fun and for hardships ... to talk about everything ... bare my soul, and have others bare their souls to me.

As a student, I know how it feels to procrastinate ... how sometimes it's hard to think about what the instructor wants you to think about.

As an employee, I know what it means to have great days ... to say same stuff, different day ... to have success ... and to screw something up.

Empathy is a concept I will endorse (forever) ... essential for continuous improvement. Empathy is a strange word. Sometimes hard to explain, hard to grasp. But I have become more aware of my own empathy, and that of others.

* * * * * * * * * * *

Empathy for Every Circumstance

Another of my students wrote an exceptional research essay built on Webster's definition of empathy as "identification with one's self with another in order to understand him better." Excerpts edited from the research paper:

Understanding someone better involves understanding his/her current feeling on a specific matter, in addition to his/her background that brought him/her to this point. Empathy involves mirroring back your perceptions of the other person's feelings until the perceptions are stated accurately.

True empathy requires an attempt to become at one with another individual.

Betsy Geedes, a consulting educator in Portland, Ore., wrote that she found in a school setting that 78 percent of the academic achievement can be traced to the quality of human interaction in the school. Roughly translated, students who feel understood and cared for, who are encouraged and have their self-concept built upon, who are in a climate of comfort, who feel good about themselves, their peers, and their teachers will achieve at higher levels.

In schools, empathy is a two-way street. Jim Fay wrote in "Teaching with Love and Logic" in 1995 of a teacher who said, "I guess if there was only one thing I could depend on it would be relationships. All the kids I work with are bigger and tougher than I am, so I can't threaten them with anything. They're not scared of anybody. So I have to rely on getting them to fall in love with me."

Her strategy rested on getting to know her students, encouraging them, and showing an interest in their activities. Many teachers think all that is needed is respect. While that is important, according to Fay's report, it is earned through friendship (empathy), not demanded.

Empathy is an important part of discipline. Using enforceable statements such as, "I accept only work that comes in on time," or "I will take the class to lunch when the room is cleaned up," empathizes with the students' need to make their own decisions and control their own lives.

Fay gave a perfect example of a teacher empathizing: "Empathizing with a student who endured the consequences of a poor choice – 'I bet you were really angry to get involved in a fight on school grounds. How long is the suspension? Three days? Well, I'll look forward to seeing you next Thursday.' – makes the behavior the 'bad guy' and the empathizing teacher a friend."

The powerful aspect of empathy, he wrote, stems from the fact that we don't want so much to be agreed with as to be understood. Empathy validates without necessarily condoning behavior. "Consequences will do the teaching," Fay wrote, "empathy will lock in the meaning."

This approach automatically rules out anger.

The language of empathy is language of respect, to build on a student's self-concept. The respect comes in the form of wording (telling students how you will act, not how they have to act), and tone of voice. Sarcasm and putdowns are never an acceptable part of empathy; when a teacher tries to control a student in this way, it usually backfires.

When the adult expresses empathy, there is no negative emotion for the youth to react to.

Empathy also surfaces in tough love. Remember Joe Clark, the principal in Patterson, N.J., who had a movie made about his tough discipline where students previously had run amok? His empathy for students was evident in all of his actions. He made the environment safe, encouraged teachers, toughened the academic standards ... and was accused of being too hard.

His most memorable line of empathy was, "It is a betrayal of the child to pass him without knowledge of the basics. You think repeating a grade is hard on him? How about life as an illiterate? How easy do you think that is?"

Empathy does not mean responding in soft ways ... just with an understanding attitude.

Books abound that illustrate the value of empathy in all relationships, especially familial. Several authors have delved into the gender differences *("Men Are From Mars,*

Women Are From Venus"; "You Just Don't Understand Me") ... and empathy is an important element in every one of Stephen Covey's *"Seven Habits of Highly Effective People."*

His fifth habit is "Seek First to Understand, Then to Be Understood: Principles of Empathetic Communication."

Covey stresses that empathy is first of all an internal quality, an attitude of loving, caring, oneness with the participants in your life. Empathy with one's self is at the root of empathy for others. He says, "Developing the inward quality of empathy is foundational to the outward expression of it. Empathy is essential to the wise creation of priorities in anyone's life since helpful personal relationships are such an important part of one's personal and public life."

In order to have true empathy, whatever is important to another person must become equally important to you.

In Loving Memory of Rogelio

His mother cries.
Police sirens echo.
A young boy dies ...
Newsman says it's sad, he says it shouldn't have been,
But he really don't care, it wasn't his friend.
The world ain't going to stop to remember you, Rogelio,
Even though we want it to ...
A generation of hopeless youth is what we all share.
Born dying, it seems, and none but us cares.
When it comes down to it, all you've got is your
family and friends.
And you never know how close you are
till one's life ends.
No one understands us, nor how we show love by
painting your name on a wall,
But no one doesn't matter, their friend didn't fall.
So when I drink, I'll pour some on the curb,
And when I think, your laughter will be heard.
You'll never be forgotten, Rogelio, we'll remember you
for all our years.
And now I pray you hear this poem,
cause through this poem
I shed my tears.

—John Cornett, a student

6

Accept Each and Every Person as a Worthy Human Being

There is so much good in the worst of us, and so much bad in the best of us, that it behooves all of us not to talk about the rest of us.

—*Robert Louis Stevenson*

Theme: Accept each and every person as a worthy human being, even if you do not approve of or condone things they say or do.

The length of a person's hair, his or her environment, background, problems, social status, title – none of these should influence whether you accept someone as a worthy human being. Once you accept all people as they are, you will notice a definite improvement in your communication skills.

Keep in mind that acceptance and approval are distinctively different. You are not required to agree with a person's behavior or way of thinking. Your willingness to accept people as worthy human beings opens the door to them reciprocating, accepting you.

This concept is summed up in a popular phrase: harmony in a world of differences.

Total acceptance is difficult, because each of us has ideas about what is acceptable or unacceptable based on values we have developed within our respective environments. But easy and hard are not the issues; if we are to make headway in dealing with alienated youths, total acceptance (not approval) of them in their current human condition is essential.

Gerald Jampolsky in his work, *Love is the Answer,* demonstrates just how hard it is by challenging us to go through one full day without passing judgment on another person for what they say or do. Try it.

* * * * * * * * * * *

We usually become aware of a person's behavior before we are aware of where they are coming from. Habitually, we do not pause to consider their perceptions of the world around them, based on their values – however misguided we may judge them to be. Also keep in mind that people are not always fully aware of what is going on inside or around them.

This is important to consider because our conditioning is to immediately judge behavior as appropriate (right) or inappropriate (wrong) – to make value judgments.

Individuals most often have a differing point of view on the same issue. You and I can look at the same situation, or individual, and see something totally different, depending on how we filter what we see through our value system.

The great Mahatma of India, Mohandas Gandhi, said, "What might appear to be truth to one might not appear to be truth to another. That never bothers the seeker of truth."

When you first glance at this sketch, what do you see? Perhaps you see a vase, or goblet.

You're right.

Oops. Perhaps you see two faces.

You're right.

Both perceptions are correct, of course, and this illustrates the importance of remaining open to consideration of another person's point of view that differs from yours.

The difficulty arises when another person's values and way of thinking conflict with yours as you view the same circumstances or situation.

* * * * * * * * * * * *

To break down the barriers, strive to get to know the other person to some degree. Speak to her or him in an honest, non-exploitative, caring, concerned manner. Be *human* and allow her or him to be human, with all the frailty and vulnerability that being human encompasses.

I often hear the complaint when a teacher or principal reaches out to a troubled student, "I'd like to get to know you, but I'm not sure how." Attitude is the starting point; you must want to get to know the student, remain open to hearing and understanding the student's point of view, and then acknowledge and accept it without immediately reacting on harsh judgment.

With this understanding atmosphere, you give individuals the opportunity to confide significant information about themselves. The result is greater trust, thereby opening the door for a substantial relationship to develop instead of a stand-off. As two persons — *i.e.*, teacher and student — continue to share experiences and relate to one another, they grow to know and trust and create the possibility of a positive, lasting relationship based on empathy and acceptance.

EXERCISE 1

CHECK LIST FOR GETTING TO KNOW ANOTHER PERSON

This exercise, involving two persons, facilitates getting to know someone on a more personal level. Complete the open-ended statements at whatever level of self-disclosure you and the other person are comfortable with. Follow these ground rules in completing the exercise:

1. Keep all information strictly confidential.
2. Work on the statements in order; avoid looking ahead.
3. Both of you responds to each statement before continuing to the next one.
4. Either party can decline to respond to any statement or question.
5. If either partner becomes obviously uncomfortable or anxious, stop the exercise. Either of you can call off the exchange of information at any time.

Start now:

1. My name is...
2. My main interests in life are ...
3. The best movie I have seen recently (or the best book I have read recently) is ...
4. Right now I am feeling ...

Checkpoint: The most important skill in getting to know another person is *listening*. To check your ability to understand what one another is communicating, both of you go through the following steps:

A. Decide which of you will speak first.
B. The first speaker completes the following in two or three sentences: *When I think about the future I see myself ...*
C. The second person then repeats what the first person said. The first person must be satisfied that he or she has been heard accurately, or else require rephrasing until the partner gets it correct.
D. Change places and repeat the exercise.

Resume the original exercise:

1. When I am in a new group I …
2. When I enter a room filled with people I usually feel …
3. When I feel anxious in a new situation I usually …
4. In groups, I feel most comfortable when the leader …
5. Social norms make me feel …
6. I am happiest when …
7. What turns me on most is …
8. When I am rejected I usually …
9. To me, belonging is …
10. What turns me off most is …
11. When I am alone I usually …
12. In crowds I …
13. To me, taking orders from another person …
14. I am rebellious when …

Checkpoint: Have a 2-3 minute discussion about the experience so far. Maintain eye contact. Cover the following points:

A. How well are you listening?
B. How open and honest have you been?
C. How eager (or not) are you to continue?
D. Do you feel you are getting to know each other?

Resume the original exercise:

1. The emotion I find most difficult to control is …
2. My weakest point is …
3. I love …

4. I am afraid of ...
5. I believe in ...
6. I am most ashamed of ...
7. The thing I like best about you is ...
8. You are ...
9. I think you would most like to know ...
10. I am ...

When you have finished, you should be able to look at this person you didn't know in a more accepting, open-minded, and non-judgmental way.

* * * * * * * * * *

Another road block to acceptance and open communication is stereotyping. Often we automatically reject a person because of bias or prejudice about outward appearance, never tapping into how he or she feels or thinks. Consider the following stereotypes, and how you respond to them:

- Female in tight jeans, tight sweater, and rings on every finger.
- Young persons with hoops or studs in their ears, nose, lips, and/or eyebrows (or elsewhere).
- Male with a mustache, scraggly beard, and long hair.
- 4th-5th grade girl wearing heavy makeup.
- Male wearing an earring in one ear.
- Person wearing cowboy boots, jeans jacket, and cowboy hat.
- Obese person with unkempt appearance.

- Person in designer clothing.
- Person wreaking of alcohol or marijuana.
- Two persons of the same sex walking hand-in-hand.
- Person driving a fancy sports car.
- Person driving a pick-up truck.
- Person who plays in a rock band.
- Grade school or junior high student smoking and loitering in the shopping mall.
- Person with a smirk or cocky grin.
- Cheerleader or pom-pom girl who becomes pregnant.
- Person disinterested in sports and anti-jock.

List some stereotypes of your own on which you have passed automatic judgment. In summary, place emphasis on the importance of expressing empathy in dealing with individuals. Show an insightful, subjective, non-critical awareness of other persons' feelings and emotions. An effective, helping person communicates in a non-defensive, non-threatening, genuine manner, revealing openness and acceptance and a sincere effort to legitimize and understand another person's world and point of view.

7

Provide Loving Care and Concern for Others

Love is patient and kind; love is not jealous, or conceited, or proud; love is not ill-mannered, or selfish, or irritable; love does not keep a record of wrongs; love is not happy with evil, but is happy with truth.

— Corinthians 13, the Holy Bible

Theme: Provide much tender loving care and genuine concern for others.

To love and be loved is a basic human need. Love encompasses our need to be seen, heard, touched, recognized, and appreciated.

Some behaviorists suggest that we each have an inborn need for love, togetherness, and human interaction. An experiment once divided two groups of infants. Group 1 received good nutrition and vitamins, but not personal love. Group 2 received the same food and supplements, plus human love and nurturing. Group 2 grew faster emotionally and physically. The most startling conclusion from the study was that some of Group 1 actually were on the verge of death before changes were made in love and nurturing.

The need for love and nurturing does not go away, and in fact probably increases, with adolescence and adulthood. A familiar saying is that three major ingredients lead to happiness – something meaningful to do, something meaningful to look forward to, and someone to love.

It is never too late to give or accept love. Genuine care and concern for others – *i.e.*, agape, or what is commonly called brotherly love – can begin instantly, now. Your approval and unconditional love means a great deal to a person of any age.

Love is energy. Love is a creative, self-perpetuating, healthy force. The time is now to focus on our love energy needs. We need to produce love in abundance so, like other forms of energy, we can store it, yet use it continually and let it flow spontaneously. Love begets love.

Think of love as a piece to life's puzzle. Have you noticed how jigsaw puzzle fans dump all the pieces on a table, turn them all right side up, and then slowly fit them together? Methodically, the puzzle takes shape until the last piece is in place. If a piece turns up missing, the picture is out of balance.

Life consists of a daily process of fitting the pieces of a puzzle together. If love is missing, the picture will never be completed.

* * * * * * * * * * *

Human love comprises five dimensions:

- Intensity
- Extensity
- Duration
- Purity
- Adequacy

The *intensity* of love is less when performing a courageous act than when risking your life for someone.

The *extensity* of love ranges from the extent of love for self or family to love of all humankind.

The *duration* of love might be momentary, such as when a soldier briefly risks life for a comrade and later becomes disassociated. Or, it might be a life-long commitment, such as a friendship or marriage.

The *purity* of love at its highest level is without exploitation, but if love is merely a means to an end, the purity level stands at ground zero.

The *adequacy* of love is substantive when the subjective goal and objective consequences are identical or compatible. To illustrate: Some parents love their children, yet the children become spoiled, irresponsible, or dishonest. The aim of the love reaps undesirable consequences, therefore is inadequate.

* * * * * * * * * *

EXERCISE 2

Use this graph to measure your LOVE QUOTIENT:

Make a dot on the numbered line that best reflects your loving quotient in each dimension.

100____

80 ____

60 ____

40 ____

20 ____

0 ____

Intensity Extensity Duration Purity Adequacy

Draw a line connecting the dots. Then ask yourself:

- Am I satisfied or dissatisfied with my loving ability? Why?
- What am I willing to do to increase my love quotient?
- When am I going to start?
- How will I follow through and be accountable?

Now try the experiment again, repeatedly, with specific individuals in mind (spouse, offspring, sibling, parent, student, peer, etc.), and ask yourself:

- What differences do I notice?
- In what areas do I need to focus additional love energy?
- What steps do I need to take to achieve my goals?

* * * * * * * * * *

THE TENDER LOVING CARE CONSTITUTION

1. People have a fundamental right to be loved. Things are to be used; people are to be loved.
2. The ways to love are many. Love can be a smile, a wink, a compliment, praise, simply talking and listening to people, sharing in activities, having fun, being fun, seeking the positive, teaching people how to make their own sunshine.
3. Love is unconditional — I love you because you're you. Let people know you love them no matter what. Love is the most important gift you can give. Provide unconditional love so when problems arise, a person can turn to you instead of drugs, crime, or suicide.
4. Love is patient and kind ... never jealous or envious, boastful or proud, haughty or selfish. Love does not demand its own way. Love is not irritable or touchy. Love does not hold grudges and will hardly notice when others do wrong. Love is never glad about injustice, but rejoices whenever truth wins out.
5. Discipline is love. Always compliment before criticizing. Set standards. Boundaries provide security. Be firm, yet positive. If God had wanted us to be permissive, he would have given 10 Suggestions rather than 10 Commandments.
6. Have faith in yourself, fellow humans, and God. Faith gives purpose to life.

PUT ANOTHER NAIL IN THE COFFIN

You went to class without paper or pen.
You're in big trouble for that major sin.
Put another nail in the coffin
You're one minute late
Because your kidneys can't wait.
Put another nail in the coffin
You skipped class without a pass
To do your work for another class.
Put another nail in the coffin
Basketball and track is where you thrive
But you can't play because you didn't pass five.
Put another nail in the coffin
You can't sit still.
Eight hours wears down the will.
Put another nail in the coffin
Too many teachers have forgotten to care.
Too many teachers have no time to spare.
Put another nail in the coffin
How many lives will have to be lost?
Saving them is just too great a cost.
Put another nail in the coffin
Around the grave we will all stand
With tears in our eyes and tissue in hand
As we put the nails in the coffin.

— *By Joyce Bright, a graduate student*

8

Develop a Positive Self-Image

He who reigns within himself, and rules passions, desires, and fears, is more than a king.

—John Milton

Theme: Develop a positive self-image and use a positive approach when dealing with people.

Your self-concept forms the center of your universe, your frame of reference, your personal reality, and your special vantage point for living.

Self-concept is a filter through which you see, hear, evaluate, and understand all that occurs in your world. How you see and feel about yourself has a profound effect on your ability to communicate and deal with people in your life.

A strong self-concept is necessary for healthy and satisfying interactions. A weak self-concept distorts your perception of how others see and feel about you, generating strong feelings of insecurity.

Self-concept has two basic components: self-esteem and self-image.

Esteem comes from a Latin word meaning *to value highly*. Hence, to value self highly. Self-esteem is simply self-love – liking who you are, knowing that you are a unique gift of life. Self-esteem is fueled by healthy, positive self-talk. Inspirational speaker Brian Tracy says, "Say 'I like myself!' out loud 100 times a day."

Self-esteem is acknowledging your innate existence as a unique gift of life, a soul and spirit that exudes goodness.

Self-image is how you see yourself. The two play off of each other; when self-image is suffering, all the more important that strong self-esteem comes into play to offset it. A common example is a person who has gone through divorce; he or she might have an eroded image of self as a spouse, yet know that the unsuccessful marriage and divorce didn't make them a bad person and that self is still a good, decent human being (valuing self highly).

With strong self-concept you strengthen your ability to cope with your human imperfection, allowing two important dynamics to take place – making room for others to accept and appreciate you, and for you to accept and appreciate other (also imperfect) persons.

If I don't like who I am at any given time, or am down on myself for what is happening in my life, then I reduce the chances of getting along with you or anybody else. Situations and circumstances change constantly, moment to moment and place to place, and our beliefs and feelings about ourselves always will impact our communication and coping ability.

The self is the star of every act of communication. Self-concept affects the ability to communicate, and communication from others impacts on the self-concept; it's a continual juggling act. We are social creatures and we tend to derive our most crucial perceptions of self from experiences with others.

Verbal and non-verbal messages tell us whether we are liked or disliked, accepted or unacceptable, worthy of respect or disdain, and, ultimately, our image of whether we are successful or a failure. Although self-esteem comes from within, most definitely the amount of love, respect, and acceptance from others impacts on our self-concept.

A person with poor self-concept will experience difficulty conversing, expressing feelings, accepting feedback (even if it's positive), or voicing ideas that go against the grain. Such insecurity feeds the fear of being disliked. Feelings of inadequacy, inferiority, and unworthiness dilute or destroy confidence. As a result, the person thinks that his/her ideas are uninteresting or stupid, and thereby becomes guarded at best or, worse, reclusive.

The opportunity for growth in self-respect and self-improvement is essential to healthy living and effective interaction. The self is a fragile thing, harder to repair than Humpty Dumpty if shattered. Hence, positive strokes are vital, to give and to get. You never know when your smile, wink, wave, "Hi," or compliment might have the most positive impact on a person's day, or week. Or, sadly, but truly in many cases, on a whole lifetime.

Approval, praise, and attentiveness are free, so dispense them freely. The results cut both ways: you can nurture others' self-image and concept, and that behavior boomerangs to bolster yours, as well.

* * * * * * * * * *

Examine the difference in the ways the following phrases have positive and negative impact:

"I love the way you look when you comb your hair."
"It's about time you did something with that mop on top of your head."

"I'm so glad you made it to class on time. You'll not only get into less trouble, but you'll learn more, too."
"So, for once, you finally made it to class on time."

"I appreciate the way you asked for that."
"Why do you want that?"

"Eighty percent of my students completed set requirements and earned passing grades."
"I flunked 20 percent of my students!"

"He is being difficult. I move away from people when they act like that."
"You've got to learn to get along with everybody."

"Your attitude definitely has improved lately. You still have some additional work to do in that area."
"Do you always have to argue and disagree? Aren't you ever going to change?"

Write some statements of your own in positive and negative styles:

____

____

____

____

____

____

EXERCISE 3

This is an excellent self-concept recognition and development tool that is fun for any age level. For variety, you can draw pictures of, rather than write out, the responses. With drawings, you can create a Coat of Arms.

1. Write or draw two things you do really well.
2. What is your "psychological" home – the place where you feel most at ease?
3. Create your greatest success in life so far.
4. Who are the three most influential persons in your life?
5. If you had one year left to live, how would you spend the time?
6. Choose three words that you would most like to have said about you.

EXERCISE 4

Another means of finding clues to your self-concept is to complete the following statements:

1. On Saturdays I like to ...
2. If I had 24 hours to live ...
3. I feel best when people ...
4. If I had a million dollars I would ...
5. Secretly I wish ...
6. My children won't have to ...
7. If I were the president of my own company (principal of my school) ...
8. I like people who ...
9. The hardest thing for me to do is ...

After finishing the statements, go back and code them with one or more of these designations for each statement:

- P – Proud of and willing to affirm publicly.
- C – Considered another answer.
- CF – Chosen freely, without thought how others might take it.
- A – Willing to ACT on.

9

Handle Situations in a Mature Manner

Do not choose for anyone what you do not choose for yourself.

— Persian proverb

Theme: Handle situations in a mature manner, never allowing others to bring you down to their negative level.

Webster's Dictionary defines maturity: fully or highly developed, perfectly worked out; grown, ripe.

Maturity, especially emotional, is essential in dealing with conflict. We face conflict with various people virtually every day. Typically we are not aware of our maturity level for handling the conflict.

Most of our problems are people problems. When specific interactions take place and situations develop, we tend to participate in and switch back and forth in three roles:

- Victim
- Persecutor
- Rescuer

Playing out these roles creates drama determined by the maturity level of the persons interacting in the problem. Major drama occurs when somebody switches roles. The participants normally move in and out of all three roles, but each individual has a dominant, or favorite role.

As the maturity level rises, the roles disappear. Resolution of the problem becomes the core issue, not blaming, rescuing, accusing, or being Charlie Brown ("why's everybody always picking on me?").

Peruse these dialogues for insight into the various roles and levels of maturity:

> Daughter (persecutor): "You know I hate yellow. Here you went and bought me another yellow blouse."
>
> Mother (victim): "I never do anything right as far as you're concerned."
>
> Father (rescuer): "Don't you dare yell at your mother like that, young lady. Leave the dinner table, go to your room, and you are grounded."
>
> Daughter (switching to victim): "They tell me to be honest, and when I tell them what I don't like, they put me down. How can you ever please your parents?"
>
> Mother (switching to rescuer): "Don't tell your father that I brought you food. We shouldn't get so upset over a blouse, OK?"
>
> Mother (switching to persecutor, to father): "You were

tough on her. I'll bet she's sitting in her room hating you."

Father (switching to victim): "Honey, I was only trying to help you, and now you kick me where it hurts most."

Daughter (switching to rescuer): "Hey, mom, lay off! Dad's just tired."

When you gain insight into your confrontational skills in problem solving, you clearly see how you are drawn into the roles, and your maturity level rises above them. Confidence in your self-concept combines with the maturity and prevents anyone from bringing you down to their level of confrontation, giving you strength to cope much better with daily problems as they arise.

* * * * * * * * * *

A valuable tool for identifying your style in facing conflict (and offering clues to your self-concept) is the Conflict Continuum:

Confront — Defuse — Avoid

Where do you usually find yourself on this continuum?

When the sense of self-confidence and self-worth are low, or the emotional maturity quotient is low, an individual will find a proportionate difficulty in handling himself and in dealing with others during conflict.

The late Dr. Rollo May, a renowned psychologist, said that in dealing with any problem, we have three basic choices:

- Avoid it. Ignore it, hoping it will go away on its own ... which is totally ineffective, because it rarely happens.
- Leave it. That works in some situations, but often is not a viable option if the situation is at school, home, or work.
- Confront it. And confrontation means simply to deal with it, moving toward defusing and resolving – not fighting.

Close your eyes for a moment and recall a recent conflict you dealt with. Did you avoid it, on one extreme end of the spectrum? Most often, even if somehow the problem does go away without your involvement, you are left with bitterness or a grudge.

Did you confront it, at the other extreme end of the continuum? How was your maturity quotient? That is significant because your emotions rush out of control, and inappropriate behavior usually follows anger or frustration or fear (and, believe me, most everyone fears confrontation on some level).

Quick reaction and ineffective communication result from immature confrontation, usually leaving the other parties involved with bitterness or a grudge.

You are better off operating toward the middle of the spectrum, away from the extremes. Objectively assess the situation, confront it in a positive way with solutions firmly in mind, and aim for defusing. Avoidance might become necessary if others do not respond favorably to your approach. (Note: avoidance isn't bad or wrong; it just usually doesn't end the problem.)

Strong work on your confrontational and problem-solving skills bode you well in communicating and coping more effectively with troublesome situations and persons.

A common myth has it that intelligence can be measured by your ability to resolve problems, rooted in reading, writing, and computing at various levels of competence. This definition of intelligence is predicated on formal education as the true measure of self-fulfillment.

But know this: mental hospitals are filled with residents who possess all of the academic alphabet credentials (PhD, EdD, etc.) along with many who don't. A true measure of intelligence is a maturity level and self-concept that paves the way for you to live a happy life. That's why a recent book called *Emotional Intelligence* was a landmark piece of work – suggesting that EQ is as important, if not more so, than IQ.

Effective problem solving is a useful adjunct to your happiness quotient, but if you know that you can still be happy even with the inability to resolve a particular problem, *then you are truly intelligent.*

Disagreements, conflict, compromise, they are all part of what it means to be human. Consider your maturity level on the basis of how you choose to feel and respond in the face of trying circumstances. And generally we all face the same trials, such as financial distress, growing old, sickness and injury, death, accidents, natural disasters.

Why, then, do some people cope and move forward

while others collapse under the strain? Self-concept and maturity are major reasons.

Maturity is not something that just happens by the flip of the calendar. Older and wiser do not necessarily become bedfellows. You develop maturity by the way you choose to handle problems, with positive and healthy response-ability, rather than detrimental reaction.

The choice is not the other person(s) involved in the conflict.

The choice lies squarely on your shoulders.

Choose well.

EXERCISE 5

Identify and write out the scenario of a recent problem you faced. Where were you? Who was involved? How did you respond?

Where were you on the Conflict Contiuum? Were you pleased with your maturity level? Why or why not? If you were not satisfied with the results, what steps will you take to improve your EQ?

____

____

____

____

____

____

10

Be Patient and Objective When Interacting with Others

He is lifeless who is faultless.

— *Anonymous*

Theme: Observe patiently and objectively all interactions with other persons.

Webster's Dictionary defines patience: refusing to be provoked or angered, as by an insult; forbearing; tolerant; able to wait calmly for something desired; and the state, quality, or fact of being patient.

The definition of objective: having to do with known or perceived objects as distinguished from something existing only in the mind; determined by and emphasizing features and characteristics of an object (or person), rather than by thoughts and feelings; without bias or prejudice.

The two words *patient* and *objective* are key elements in developing strong listening and empathy skills. Patience and objectivity are complex concepts to implement, because of personality and emotional make-up variables among individuals.

Also, the incredible speed of life and our seeming need for instant gratification complicate matters. The pace by which we live is breaking us down physically, but even more tragic, we are destroying our minds and souls as well.

You will find it next to impossible to live a quiet existence physically and yet maintain a rapid tempo emotionally. Even an invalid can live at too high a pace. The character of our thoughts determines the pace of our lives. To slow down, we must become patient and objective.

And it behooves us to slow down before the overstimulation and super excitement becomes profoundly debilitating.

A starting point for slowing your pace is to quiet down. Practice being patient. Become more tolerant of persons and situations that you don't like or agree with. Believe that every problem has a solution. Avoid forcing an issue.

Then take note of the quieting power that wells up within you.

Practice objectivity. Assemble all facts impartially and impersonally. List all information on paper when you have time. The visual list helps clarify and crystallize your thinking, bringing the various elements of a situation into an orderly system.

Observation power overrides thinking power as your problem becomes objectified, rather than subjectified (wrought with personal biases and value judgments).

Base all decision making on rational thoughts derived from objective information gathering.

Practice being calm. Others will respond in kind. Keep

your mind relaxed so that a solution will become clear, making life less complicated.

Lao-tse, renowned Chinese philosopher, says, "Muddied water let to stand will become clear." A reading from the Tao says, "Wise people seek solutions."

And we all know the Biblical words, "Seek and you shall find." The urgent message here is to seek inner peace and calm, patiently, objectively, and slow life to a manageable crawl. The turbulence will subside accordingly.

Happy seeking.

EXERCISE 6

This requires a group of 5-6 persons with an objective of managing patience and objectivity in interacting. Choose several controversial issues to discuss, such as:

- Separation of church and state
- Legalization of abortion
- Zero population growth
- Premarital sex
- Legalization of marijuana, or other drugs
- Distribution of wealth
- College entrance requirements and testing
- Grading systems in schools
- Interracial marriage

Come up with some of your own, perhaps indigenous to your group or school or student body. Identify several stands that can be taken on each issue you select — i.e., ultra-conservative, moderate, liberal, radical, revolutionary.

It works best if participants avoid taking their own personal position. Each participant write a paragraph defending her or his selected position. Then discuss/argue/debate from that viewpoint for 10-15 minutes.

Following the group interaction, all participants write (or add to) the defense of the arbitrarily selected positions, taking a stand on their own position and viewpoint. Discuss that.

Finally, the entire group discuss observations of patience and objectivity — where they broke down, where they influenced, etc. — during the interaction on conflicting viewpoints.

11

Communicate Effectively

A person can stand up against almost anything. But he cannot stand up against uncertainties or mysteries.

— Winston Churchill

Theme: Communicate effectively ... be certain that everyone understands what you expect and what the consequences are for both met and unmet expectations.

Communication occurs through many varying channels. When a general sense of harmony, consistency, and uniformity is conveyed in messages, we take comfort in knowing what the other person said and where we stand on it.

If the message comes across as contradictory, ambivalent, vague, or unclear, we become confused, perplexed, unsure, and anxiety increases.

A small example: A mother visits her son at boarding school and gives him two neckties for his birthday, one red, one blue. The next time he comes home for dinner, the mother takes note of the blue tie he is wearing and says, "I see you're wearing the blue tie I gave you. What's the matter – didn't you like the red one?" The boy is trapped by an obscure message.

The many channels of communication create the possibility of confusion, contradiction, and negativity, even when it is not intended. Let's examine them:

- Messages we *hear:* The meaning, implication, and codes for interpretation are conveyed by tone, pitch, rhythm, inflection, speed, and accent; all in addition to the words themselves.
- Messages we *see:* Silent body language and paralanguage (clothing, automobiles, and other trappings) offer strong insight into what is going on, although not necessarily why it is going on.
- Messages we *smell:* Other animal species rely much more on this sense than humans. Still, smelling is a primitive function that sends messages to the brain not only to warn of possible danger, but to inform on such fronts as an undesirable environment, or of seductive body or cosmetic odors (perfume, etc.) that enhance sexual attraction.
- Messages we *taste:* Generally, this applies to food we ingest, linked with smell.
- Messages we *touch:* This one is extremely meaningful. You might enjoy and encourage the touch of another person, or you might recoil from it. The factors include who the person is, the softness or roughness of the touch, the circumstances (time, location), part of the body touched, the context of the touch. Is the message overt or covert? Is it clear, or does it tease? Touch often

creates some conflict, too, because most people yearn to be touched, yet we cannot exploit other people's needs when they are vulnerable.

Pay close attention to non-verbal communication. Think of someone thumbing their nose at you, smiling at you, or abruptly turning their back on you. Usually, you wouldn't need a 1,000-word discourse to understand the feelings they are expressing. At the same time, it's easy to read into those silent communications something that isn't intended.

A nose-thumbing could be clowning as well as putting down; a smile could be friendly or it could be of the "smile, and people will wonder what you're up to" variety; a back-turning could be a preoccupation or interruption by another source, as well as a snub.

Most experts on interpersonal communication say that what is NOT being said is at least as important, if not more so, than what IS being said. Non-verbal communication carries the power of conveying unstated, private thoughts and feelings even without the sender's awareness.

Watch a smoker, for example. You can determine the smoker's degree of anxiety or tension or relaxed, leisure state by the slightest non-verbal sign – tightness of the wrist in holding the cigarette.

A person who enters a room where others have gathered, hoping to appear calm and casual, might stumble awkwardly and reveal some apprehension or insecurity.

People who blush often usually are unaware of it until someone calls attention to it.

People we encounter routinely transmit instantly, as we see them for the first time, various aspects of their personalities. Most are not aware of the powerful non-verbal tip-offs they send and how it can affect your relationship, then or later.

The signals come from eye contact (or lack of it), posture, laugh or smile or frown, manner of dress – general aura derived many different ways. Do you recognize these examples of the revelations from first impressions:

- "When I shook hands with him I thought I was holding a dead fish. I felt weird."
- "I could tell immediately that she was a real person and that she liked me."
- "You could feel at once that he was angry and bitter and doesn't like people."
- "His eyes were shifty, so I realized I'd better not trust him too much."
- "She is a sparkling person with a glowing spirit."
- "He looked like a warm, friendly person, I immediately felt comfortable."
- "Did you see his (hair) (that awful beard) (those clothes)? Ewwww."

What would you say is the most significant key to improving your communication skills? I'm throwing one at you that many people don't consider: often it is simply to say a little something that could make the other person feel important!

Check List:

__ Accept all persons as worthy human beings, no better, no worse than you.

__ Show genuine interest in people.

__ Express a real concern and caring.

__ Maintain respectfulness in dealing with others...respect their human dignity, always.

__ Inspire trust and hopefulness.

__ Share a sense of humor. Always remain able to laugh at yourself, and *with* others, not *at* them.

__ Suggest possibilities, options, alternatives, and solutions to problems.

__ Sustain an optimistic, positive outlook. See the glass as half full, not half empty.

__ Abide by boundaries and limitations, yours and theirs. Those can be physical, spiritual, emotional, cultural, religious, etc.

__ Help individuals see that they have done the best they could so far, in view of their life background and experiences, but that they might be able to do more in the future if they can keep from giving up.

NOTE FROM A SUICIDAL STUDENT

"My life was filled with drama, because I made it that way. But it was also filled with hurt, anger, anxiety, frustrations, and loneliness. But most of all it was filled with confusion. So anyone who has these kinds of problems, talk about them. It works miracles. Ask me, I know. But it's nothing to be proud of."

12

Listen Carefully to What People Say

Create in me, O God, a loving and listening heart.
— *Psalms*

Theme: Listen carefully to what people say. In response, avoid lecturing or moralizing.

Traditionally, education about communication skills centers on self-expression. Research substantiates that *listening* has been under-emphasized as a powerful tool for enhancing effective communication between two or more humans. In keeping with the theme of parenting and teaching with empathy, the good listener who *truly hears* – that is, acknowledges and legitimizes what another person says, with empathy and compassion, is more valued and appreciated than the merely good *talker*.

Our tendency, woefully, is to listen only to what we consider important, that which fits our wants and needs and satisfaction, and to tune out anything else. If, in fact, we tuned in at all.

You must keep in mind at all times that other people's reality, their problems and situations, are of utmost importance to them, just as yours is with you.

Listening is more intricate and complicated than just hearing. Listening is an art, to be developed with practice, patience, understanding, and objectivity. While you hear with your ears, listening integrates physical, emotional, and intellectual processes in a search for meaning and comprehension.

Effective listening occurs when you can discern and translate the sender's message accurately and within intended context. When this occurs, communication is achieved.

Listening is a proactive activity, not passive. Good listening does not occur casually.

Practice broadening your listening skills:

- Suspend judgment, at least temporarily.
- Develop purpose and commitment to listening well.
- Avoid distractions, such as noise, views, other people, and focus on the speaker, maintaining good eye contact.
- Pause and reflect before responding.
- Develop paraphrasing in your own words and context about what you hear, and then review the central themes of the message for correctness.
- Reflect mentally on what the speaker is trying to say.
- Prepare to respond when the speaker indicates a readiness for comments.

Feelings and attitude can affect your perceptions as a listener. How you feel about yourself — that all-important self-concept again – and how you feel about the person sending the message will impact on how well you listen.

As a listener, keep in mind:

- Be fully accessible to the person talking. If you are preoccupied, or your mind wanders, or you attempt to do something else at the same time, you decrease your chances of hearing and understanding efficiently. Comedian Woody Allen had a famous line: "It is hard to hum a tune and contemplate one's own death at the same time."

You also surely have experienced the sinking feelings when you are talking to someone in, say, their office at work or school, and they continue to work without looking up as you speak. Or, at the table at home, when a parent or sibling continues to read the paper or watch TV when you try to tell them something important to you.

- Remain aware of your feelings during the listening process. Emotions and reactions such as anger, disdain, defensiveness, and prejudice typically crop up, and they definitely distort your listening ability.

Another effective way of responding in a listening situation is called "active" listening. It means you assume responsibility to understand the content and context of what is being said to you. It involves responding with a statement in your own words, essentially repeating back what you believe the person talking meant.

Example: "The deadline for this report is not realistic."
Your response: "I'm hearing you say you feel pressure to get the report finished."
The first person then can either affirm that you heard, or restate the comment.

Basically, this involves putting yourself in the other person's place. Feeding back your perceptions allows the listener to quickly check accuracy of meaning and understanding. This leaves no room for misinterpretation after the fact. You therefore avoid that famous line: "You didn't hear what I said."

Active listening creates a climate for open communication that produces positive results and satisfaction for all parties involved in the conversation. The good listener learns to "see" what a person means, and how that person feels about situations and problems.

Active listening communicates acceptance and increases trust.

A caution flag: the process is not intended to manipulate people to behave or think the way you think they should. You do not read things into what they are saying. Nor do you "parrot" the exact words back. Empathy is a necessary ingredient.

Bad timing is another possible pitfall. Active listening is not appropriate in a rush. You must make and take time to help address a person's expressed concerns. Also, active listening is inappropriate when someone is seeking just factual information that requires no empathetic feedback.

Finally, it is important in active listening to be sensitive to non-verbal messages about the right time to stop giving feedback.

A word about non-words: listen for deeper meaning behind the words spoken – hear the feeling, hear what is NOT being said.

The power of that concept came home to me in a harsh way in an essay that was shared with me.

Please Hear What I'm Not Saying

Don't be fooled by me.

Don't be fooled by the face I wear.

For I wear a mask. I wear a thousand masks, masks that I'm afraid to take off, and none of them are me.

Pretending is an art that's second nature to me. But don't be fooled.

I give you the impression that I am secure, that all is sunny and unruffled with me, within, as well as without. That confidence is my name and coolness my game, that the water's calm and I'm in command, and that I need no one.

But don't believe me.

Please.

My surface may be smooth, but my surface is my mask, my varying and ever-concealing mask.

Beneath lies no smugness, no complacence.

Beneath it dwells the real me, in confusion and fear, in aloneness. But I hide this, I don't want anybody to know it.

That's why I frantically create a mask to hide behind. A nonchalant, sophisticated facade, to help me pretend, to shield me from the glance that knows.

But such a glance is precisely my salvation.

And I know it. That is, if it's followed by acceptance, if it is followed by love.

It's the only thing that can liberate me, from myself, from my own self-built prison walls, from the barriers that I so painstakingly erect.

It's the only thing that will assure me of what I can't assure myself, that I'm really worth something.

But I don't tell you this. I don't dare. I'm afraid to.

I'm afraid that your glance will not be followed by love.

I'm afraid that you'll think less of me. That you'll laugh.

And your laugh would kill me.

I'm afraid that deep down I'm nothing, that I'm just no good, and that you will see this and reject me.

So I play my game, with a facade of assurance without, and a trembling child within.

And so begins the parade of masks, the glittering but empty parade of masks.

And my life becomes a front.

I idly chatter to you in the suave tones of surface talk.

I tell you everything that's really nothing, and nothing of what's everything, of what's crying within me.

So, when I'm going through my routine, please don't be fooled by what I'm saying.

Please listen carefully, and try to hear what I'm not saying, and what I'd like to say.

Honestly.

I dislike the superficial game I'm playing, the superfi-

cial phony game.

I'd really like to be genuine and spontaneous and me – but you've got to help me.

You've got to hold out your hand, even when that's the last thing I seem to want or need.

Only you can wipe away from my eyes the blank stare of the breathing dead.

Only you can call me into aliveness.

Each time you're kind, and gentle, and encouraging; each time you try to understand because you really care, my heart begins to grow wings, very small wings, very feeble wings, but wings.

With your sensitivity and sympathy, and your power of understanding, you can breath life into me. I want you to know that.

I want you to know how important you are to me, how you can be a creator of the person that is me, if you choose to.

Please choose to.

You alone can break down the wall behind which I tremble. You alone can remove my mask. You alone can release me from my shadow world of panic and uncertainty, from my lonely prison.

So do not pass me by.

It will not be easy for you.

A long conviction of worthlessness builds strong walls.

The nearer you approach me, the blinder I may strike back.

It's irrational. But despite what the book says about man, I am irrational.

I fight against the very thing I cry out for.

But I am told that love is stronger than strong walls.

In this lies my hope.

My only hope.

Please try to beat down these walls with firm hands, but with gentle hands, for a child is very sensitive.

Who am I, you may wonder.

I am someone you know very well.

I am every man you meet.

I am every woman you meet.

13

React... But Avoid Over-Reacting to Situations

Life is not what happens to you, but how you react to what happens to you that makes the difference!

—*Dr. Robert Schuller*

Theme: React ... but avoid over-reacting by remembering you are responsible for your behavior in managing situations.

Anger and violence seem to be the order of the day – in homes, schools, and work environments all over the country. News headlines every morning in the paper and every night on TV suggest that America is on a rampage, from road rage to school shootings to random killings in neighborhoods everywhere.

To deal effectively with the rise in negative stress, the frustrations and anger of everyday life, we must – absolutely *must* – examine our coping skills, or seeming lack thereof.

By developing potential for coping with an increasingly hostile culture, you can turn the tide. You can learn what is popularly called "response-able" behavior, and displace irresponsible, reactive, and destructive over-reaction.

First, engage in a survey that will provide insight into your proclivity for over-reacting, even to a point of turning violent:

EXERCISE 7

For each question, circle the number under the word that best describes your answer. Specific instructions at the end of the quiz will tell you how to total your score and what it means.

STRESS

Stress is the physical or emotional reaction that you experience when events or circumstances cause you to adapt. Think of the changes, challenges, disappointments, important decisions or assignments in your life.

	Most of the time	**Fre-quently**	**Some-times**	**Seldom**	**Never**	**Do not have a problem**
1. Do you think that stress in your life is mostly caused by what other people do?	4	3	2	1	0	0
2. Do you think your actions and decisions are the cause of your stress?	4	3	2	1	0	0
3. Are you worried about whether you are going to be successful?	4	3	2	1	0	0
4. Are you concerned about the amount of stress in your life?	4	3	2	1	0	0
5. Have you found ways of dealing with your stress?	0	0	1	2	3	4
6. Have you asked for help to relieve the source of your stress?	0	0	1	2	3	4

ANGER

Anger is a strong feeling that you experience when events are threatening. Managing anger depends upon taking responsibility for one's own emotions and resisting the temptation to harbor blame, fury or silent resentment. Think of situations that have made you angry.

	Most of the time	**Fre-quently**	**Some-times**	**Seldom**	**Never**	**Do not have a problem**
1. Is your anger usually in response to the actions of others?	4	3	2	1	0	0
2. Do you get angry when little things go wrong?	4	3	2	1	0	0
3. Do you let your anger show impulsively?	4	3	2	1	0	0
4. Do you react suddenly when you feel angry?	4	3	2	1	0	0
5. Do you talk to someone when things go wrong?	0	0	1	2	3	4
6. Have you tried to figure out what was threatening when you were angry?	0	0	1	2	3	4

HOSTILITY

Hostility is the storing up of anger in indirect ways that are destructive. Studies conclude that people who scored high on a hostility scale were one and a half times more likely to have a heart attack than those who had lower scores. Hostility often is a byproduct of frustration and high stress levels. Think of situations that have frustrated or irritated you.

	Most of the time	Fre-quently	Some-times	Seldom	Never	Do not have a problem
1. Do you feel that people are pushing you around?	4	3	2	1	0	0
2. Do you find it difficult not to argue when people disagree with you?	4	3	2	1	0	0
3. Do you try to get even whenever you can?	4	3	2	1	0	0
4. Have you broken something when you were frustrated or angry?	4	3	2	1	0	0
5. Have you looked for ways to be less grouchy or irritable?	0	0	1	2	3	4
6. Have you asked for help for your hostility or the hostility you feel from others?	0	0	1	2	3	4

ASSAULT

Assault is fighting or the willingness to use physical force against others. Generally speaking, the use of physical force to control another person is never justified. Think of times that you felt like hitting someone.

	Most of the time	Fre-quently	Some-times	Seldom	Never	Do not have a problem
1. Do you think it is okay to hit someone if you think he deserves it?	4	3	2	1	0	0
2. Has someone you care about physically hurt you when he said he was trying to teach you a lesson?	4	3	2	1	0	0
3. Have you physically hurt someone you care about when you were frustrated?	4	3	2	1	0	0
4. Have you tried to get your way by using physical force?	4	3	2	1	0	0
5. Do you have someone you can turn to when you feel like fighting?	0	0	1	2	3	4
6. Have you tried to find ways to under-stand the source of your anger?	0	0	1	2	3	4

SCORING

For each section, add the numbers that you circled. Write the subtotals here:

Stress: ________________ Anger: ________________

Hostility: ______________ Assault: ________________

WHAT YOU ANSWERS INDICATE

Zero through 6 in each category would be considered low scores. Low levels of stress, anger, hostility, and assault are indicative of individuals whose reactions to one or all of the four feelings are appropriate. You apparently have found effective outlets for relieving life's tensions. There is, however, the possibility that you are the passive recipient of others' stress, anger, hostility or assault.

Middle scores would be 7 through 18. Scores in the upper end of the middle range — 13 through 18 — often point to individuals who misdirect efforts of releasing their feelings. If you score 7 to 12 and even more so, if you score 13 to 18, now is the time to learn more effective means for dealing with stress, anger, hostility or assault. Appropriate coping techniques include being honest with yourself and examining your inner feelings, communicating your feelings to someone you trust, finding a positive physical outlet for your feelings (exercise or dance, for example), and seeking professional assistance from books, counselors, or ministers.

High scores would be those 19 to 24. High scores in any of the four areas means that you have the potential to over-react and be destructive to yourself or others.

Carefully examine your final results and speak with a trained person about your worries, fears, and concerns. Explore various alternatives available to assist you in making improvements in these areas. The sooner you take steps to make some changes, the sooner you will help yourself and others cope with common life situations more effectively. You owe it to yourself and to others to take some positive steps for improvement.

---

* * * * * * * * * *

The No. 1 emotion on the loose that we must learn to control is anger. When you fully understand where anger comes from (within, not outside), why it occurs, and what to do with it in a mature state, all other emotions will improve proportionately.

Beware of the common cop-out – "Oh, anger is natural, we're only human."

Literally, in actuality, you do not have to experience anger. Not that it is wrong, or that it makes you a bad person (although uncontrolled anger certainly will lead you to do bad things). It's just that you do not have to possess it, and when you do, you certainly do not have to languish in it and hang onto it and let it roil into rage.

Anger serves no purpose whatsoever in your quest to become a happy, fulfilled person with a good self-concept.

Anger takes the form of rage, hostility, striking out at someone verbally or physically or both, or it can simmer in glowing silence. Many euphemisms are used to deny anger, but it is not simple annoyance or irritation. Anger is immobilizing, and usually the result of wishing the world and the people in it would stop and become different on your terms.

Some people scoff at this next notion, as though anger somehow falls out of the sky, unwanted and unprovoked ... but the proven facts of behavioral study support 100 percent that anger is a choice. And people who choose it frequently fall into an anger habit.

It is a learned reaction to frustration, leading you to behave in ways you'd rather not. Severe anger is a form of insanity; you are deemed insane when you are not in control of your behavior. When you spin out of control in anger, you are temporarily insane.

No psychological reward exists for anger, and it can be debilitating. Anger produces hypertension, ulcers, rashes, heart palpitations, insomnia, fatigue, and even heart disease. Anger breaks down love relationships, interferes with communication processes, leads to guilt and depression, and is just a general nuisance that gets in your way of positive, forward-moving activity.

Many sources of anger studies say that expressing anger is healthier than keeping it bottled up inside. Yes, acknowledging that the anger is real, and expressing it, are healthier alternatives than suppression.

But the healthiest approach is eliminating anger altogether. Easy to say, hard to do. But whoever said easy was the issue? The issue is changing negative, destructive choices, habits, and behavior.

Like all emotions, anger results from a way of thinking about something, or somebody. Albert Ellis was the foremost authority on the origin of emotions. He, and many, many others since, make it clear that anger is not something that simply happens to you out of the blue. When faced with circumstances that aren't going the way you would like, you tell yourself that things shouldn't be that way (frustration, or mild anger arises).

And then you select a familiar, angry response that serves a purpose (you think), yet serves no purpose (in reality). As long as you think of anger as a part of what it means to be a human being – like there is an anger gene or something – then you justify accepting it, and avoid controlling it.

Certainly the evidence is strong that angry persons must seek non-destructive ways to vent, to let off the steam. Scream therapy is a popular way, pounding a pillow another; the best, the experts say, is vigorous physical exercise – walking, running, or other forms.

But doesn't it make sense to think of yourself as someone who can commit to eliminating anger? You can learn to think new thoughts when frustration sets in, and in immobilizing anger you displace it with more fulfilling emotions.

Annoyance, irritation, and disappointment aren't likely to go away, since the world isn't likely to suddenly become entirely the way you want it. But that hurtful emotional outburst of anger can be eliminated.

Now there's a good-news message for you!

How, you ask? Perhaps it just doesn't sound possible or feasible, from your experience. You can learn techniques such as deep breathing and relaxation, walking away from a situation, and one called "reframing" – consciously changing your thoughts about the situation. Often that takes the form of changing the thought that somebody is doing something "to" you to a thought that they simply are doing it, period, and for reasons of their own that have nothing whatsoever to do with you. When you remove yourself from being the victim, you remove the reason [cause] for anger.

A simple example would be somebody who cut you off in traffic; you take it personally, because they perhaps almost caused you to wreck or you felt threatened or afraid, and your thought is that they are a rude, irresponsible blankety-blank. Your thought could be that they were preoccupied with something that occurred in their personal life, or they needed to be somewhere in an emergency. When you "reframe" the situation, it has a calming effect.

What good does anger do you anyway? When it surfaces in a primary relationship, anger almost always will encourage the other person to continue their course of action. While the provoker might be or act afraid, he or she also knows what button to push whenever they want to.

Learn to express – and, by the way, to respond to another person's anger – with courageous new behaviors. Learn not to give power to other people's ideas and behavior that upset you. With a high self-concept and a refusal to let others control your emotional state, you won't hurt yourself with present-moment anger.

Here's a good and funny antidote: you cannot be angry and laugh at the same time. Thus, the consensus of experts is that Reader's Digest has had it right all these years – humor is the best medicine. Anger and laughter are mutually exclusive. You have the power to choose either.

When you tend to be overly sober about yourself and what you do, remind yourself that the present moment is all you have. Now is a gift; that's why they call it the present. Why waste your present being angry? Especially when laughing feels so good.

Practice laughing just for the sake of laughing. You don't have to have a reason to laugh. Just do it. Observe yourself and others in this nutty world, and decide whether carrying around anger serves you best, or whether a sense of humor about it all will give you one of the most priceless gifts of all – laughter.

It feels so good. And isn't feeling good what we're all after?

Laughter is the sunshine of the soul. Without sunshine nothing lives or grows.

CHECKLIST FOR ANGER RECOGNITION AND MANAGEMENT

Do you chose to be angry…

___ in your automobile

___ in a competitive game

___ about taxes

___ over tardiness of others

___ at the disorganization or sloppiness of others
___ over the loss or damage of possessions
___ over things people say or believe
___ over world events beyond your control
___ over a child doing his or her job – being a child?

List other conditions that get your goat:

____

____

Checklist for the forms in which anger is displayed:

___ Abusive language
___ Ridiculing
___ Sarcasm
___ Physical violence (spanking, fist-fighting, or worse)
___ Emotional violence (instilling fear)
___ Glowering
___ Ignoring (the infamous silent treatment)
___ Temper tantrums
___ Phrases like, "He infuriates me," or "You really aggravate me." (This blames somebody else for your anger, therefore giving them power over you.)

List others you have experienced:

____

____

____

Before coming to grips with your anger, you must recognize the catalysts for choosing it. Some psychological motives for becoming angry:

- Whenever you lose self-control, anger directs the responsibility for how you feel to a person or event, rather than you taking personal responsibility for it.
- Anger helps manipulate persons who fear you, such as spouse, children, students, or people who report to you at work.
- Anger draws attention, making you feel powerful and important. No question, it can be addictive and feel good to be mad.
- Anger is a handy exercise. You can go insane, temporarily, and then excuse yourself by saying, "I couldn't help it."
- You can get your way because others would rather placate or avoid you than have to put up with the exhibition.
- You can disrupt and break down communication in which you feel threatened because someone else is more skillful.
- You don't have to work on yourself when you can hide behind anger. It's their fault, their problem, not yours.
- You can wallow in self pity after an anger attack.
- You can excuse losing or poor performance with a simple fit of temper.
- Fear of intimacy or love creates what one expert called "the dance of anger," because in anger you can avoid sharing yourself affectionately or with vulnerability. While angry, you don't let your guard down.

With commitment and practice, you can improve on giving in to anger. Most likely it will require a great deal of new thinking, and you must work on one present moment at a time. Chose specific strategies for attacking anger:

- First, and most important, get in touch with your thoughts at the moment of anger. Awareness is paramount to changing the pattern.
- Postpone anger. Count to 10, breathe deep, then to 15, then 20. Once you see that you can, indeed, put off anger, you learn to control it habitually.
- When using anger purposefully in the guise of instructing a child, fake the anger. Raise your voice and look stern, but fend off the emotional experience, the pain of anger.
- Avoid deluding yourself into believing that you enjoy something that you find distasteful.
- Ask someone that you trust to help, someone professionally-trained if necessary.
- Keep an anger journal. Record the exact time, place, and circumstances.
- Move physically close to someone you love at the moment of your anger.
- Talk about your anger with persons who most often feel its wrath, but at a time when you are not angry.
- In a relationship, defuse anger by labeling how you feel and how you believe your partner feels during the first 10, crucial, seconds.
- Get rid of expectations you have for others, a source of disappointment that sets you up. When the expectations go away, so will the anger.

- Remind yourself constantly that children will always be active and loud, and getting angry about it won't change it.
- In a traffic jam, time yourself. See how long you can go without exploding. This is an excellent situation in which to work on emotional control.

* * * * * * * * * *

Anger gets in the way. It is good for nothing. It only allows you to justify how upset you feel by blaming conditions outside of yourself.

Develop a positive self-concept, learn to control your anger, and you will be well on the way to responding well to problematic situations, rather than over-reacting and boiling over.

A SHORT COURSE IN HUMAN RELATIONS

The **six** most important words:
"I admit I made a mistake."

The **five** most important words:
"You did a good job."

The **four** most important words:
"What is your opinion?"

The **three** most important words:
"If you please."

The **two** most important words:
"Thank you."

The **least** important word:
"I."

14

Be Firm, Fair, Consistent, and Honest

Who is strong? He that can conquer his bad habits.
— Poor Richard's Almanac, by Benjamin Franklin

Theme: Successful personal interactions are best achieved by being firm, fair, consistent, and honest.

Controlling skills are essential to successful human interaction. This is not to be confused with *control*, as in power and control demands that create barriers and breakdown in communication.

I use the term controlling in the context of maintaining a disciplined style – the ability to discipline yourself and set discipline guidelines for others.

The techniques are useful to administrators, in education or business, and to teachers, supervisors, parents – anyone in a role that requires maintaining control of a group and its environment. That can be a classroom, a family, an office, a team.

Controlling and discipline are often perceived as negative traits. They conjure mental images of rapped knuckles, dunce caps, hickory sticks or paddles from another, more restrictive era of education and parenting. Today, among frustrated educators, parents and students, the image might be of shouts, commands, reprimands, threats, denials, deprivations, and other harsh utterances and actions.

Discipline does not have to connote negativity. A positive approach to discipline, indeed, reaps surprisingly wonderful results. The positive application of discipline is rooted in firmness, fairness, consistency, and honesty.

* * * * * * * * * *

Firmness requires communicating in a direct, straightforward, no-nonsense manner. Firm, yes; threatening, no. Firm, yes; demeaning and despotic, no. An ambivalent approach causes uncertainty and confusion about the expectations and consequences of behavior.

Whomever you deal with, he or she must know that you are in charge, and that you are taking action in the best interest of all involved parties at all times. Everyone deserves to fully and clearly understand the consequences if your expectations are not met, and the benefits if they are met.

This does not mean you have the right to dehumanize in any way. Maintain respect for human dignity at all times, regardless of the severity and unacceptability of the situation.

Fairness takes us back to the material on listening. Controlling fairly means listening to all sides of a story. Often things are not as they might appear at first. Circumstantial evidence can be overwhelming.

A challenge to your fairness quotient arises when you disapprove of certain individuals because of their appearance or mannerisms, but they deserve the same fair treatment as persons who fit your ideal image. Regardless of age, gender, appearance, background, ability, title, or social status, gather information objectively, without bias.

When you are fair, the people you deal with will accept and respect you, even though you control (and perhaps restrict) their environment and choices.

Maintaining *consistency* means remaining free from variation in your day-to-day personality and application of discipline. People in your world find it very perplexing if one day you are pleasant, easy-going, and willing to bend the rules, and the next day you are grouchy, irritable, and just lying in wait for someone to step out of line.

Persons of all ages can accept your personality, whatever it may be, as long as they know what to anticipate. The famed philosopher Joseph Campbell said, "The privilege of a lifetime is being who you are." Be yourself. It will serve you well.

Actually, it is very difficult to be something you are not. If you are a grouch, then be a grouch seven-24. If you are pleasant, show up pleasant around the clock.

Operating from an *honest* foundation means realizing that you will deal with nobody who is or ever will be perfect. That includes you. In the course of a conversation, if a subject arises of which you know little or nothing, admit it. If you use bad judgment in a disciplinary situation, admit it.

Criticizing a person before you have walked in their

shoes will cause you to lose respect and communicative credibility. If you are open and honest, revealing your flaws and being vulnerable, you allow the persons in your life to reciprocate with honesty.

Another facet of honesty is admitting that no single person has experienced all things. You don't have to be bitten by a rattlesnake to know the bite is poisonous and fatal. In our ever-changing world, none of us can be expected to stay abreast – let alone be an expert – on all developments.

EXERCISE 8

List personal goals for improving your controlling skills (setting the boundaries of discipline), based on the four main ingredients:

Be firm ______________________________________

____

____

____

Be fair ______________________________________

____

____

____

Be consistent ______________________________

____

____

____

Be honest ______________________________

____

____

____

A PRIMER ON GETTING ALONG WITH PEOPLE

1. Keep a tight rein on your tongue. Always say less than you think. Cultivate a low, persuasive voice.
2. Make promises sparingly. Keep them faithfully, no matter what it costs.
3. Never let an opportunity pass to say a kind and encouraging word to or about somebody. Praise good work, regardless of who did it. If feedback (criticism) is necessary, apply it helpfully, never with spite.
4. Take an interest in others — their pursuits, work, family. Make merry with those who rejoice, and with those who weep, mourn. Let everyone you meet, however humble, know that s/he is a person of importance.
5. Be cheerful. Dwelling on your minor aches and small disappointments only burdens or depresses those around you. Everyone is carrying some kind of load.
6. Keep an open mind. Discuss, avoid arguing. A superior mind is able to disagree without being disagreeable.
7. Let your virtues speak for themselves. Refuse to talk about another person's vices. Discourage gossip.
8. Be careful of other people's feelings. Wit and humor at someone's expense can be unexpectedly hurtful and is not worthwhile.
9. Pay no attention to ill-natured remarks about you. The person who delivered the message is not the most accurate reporter in the world. Simply live so that nobody can believe what they said. Back-biting leads to nervous disorders and indigestion.
10. Display no eagerness for any credit you feel you are due. Perform your best and exercise patience. Forget about yourself. Others will remember your contribution, making success all the sweeter.

15

Analyze the Personality with Which You Are Dealing

My business is not to remain myself, but to make the absolute best of what God made.

— *Robert Browning*

Theme: No single method or style works for all people. Analyze the person with whom you are dealing, and adapt your personality accordingly.

I firmly believe, firmly, because of my experiences and results, that if you implement the philosophy and techniques of this body of work, you will experience a big boost in your ability to communicate, cope, and take control of your environment.

The suggestions and exercises herein are applicable universally across the spectrum of age, personalities, cultural differences, and exceptionalities. As with any methodology, adaptations must apply in differing circumstances.

Yet, I also know that the core philosophy I have laid out will not solve all of your problems or work with all people. Everyone whom you encounter is involved in the same search for life's meaning, for self-fulfillment, and happiness. And so many and varied offerings are available that it is mind-boggling and sometimes confusing, if not conflicting.

While one person might swear by Stephen Covey's program rooted in his *Seven Habits of Highly Successful People,* another might be neck-deep in *The Course in Miracles* by Helen Schucman. My experiences and studies run the gamut across the philosophies of meditation, behavior modification, Rogerian counseling, transactional analysis, bio-feedback, hypnosis, reality therapy, yoga, and many others.

One of the keys to successfully dealing with people – especially troubled and troublesome persons who create unique difficulties – is the ability to analyze your own personality and style and adapt it to the personality and style with whom you are interacting.

To raise your self-awareness, engage in a modified form of transactional analysis:

The starting point is an assumption that all persons have three components within their personality, known as ego states and labeled *Parent, Adult,* and *Child.*

The *Parent* in you feels and behaves similarly to your mother, father, or whoever raised you. Your inner Parent can be critical or caring, or both.

Your *Adult* is your built-in computer; it processes facts to base decisions on.

The *Child* ego state maintains the same feelings and behavior patterns from when you were very young, from infancy into elementary school age.

The Child can be free to act on its own, away from the influence of the internal Parent. Or, the Child might adapt to please the Parent.

Often, the three ego states operate in conflict with one another. You've no doubt heard, or said, "Part of me wants to..." That is quite common. The voices of the Three You's speak to you from different vantage points.

You usually are best off listening to your Adult.

The Parent echoes your shoulds and oughts. The voice says, "You must do this," or offers "Don't" slogans like, "If you want something done right, do it yourself," or "a woman's place is in the home," or "boys will be boys." It is the voice of deep-seated values, all about right and wrong, good and bad.

The Child typically says, "I want what I want when I want it." Or, "try to make me."

The Adult operates as the voice of reason. It prefers to decide based on facts, not feelings. It says, "Here is how this works," and considers what the probabilities are in certain behaviors.

Tune in to these voices within you for clues to your behavior and style in decision-making and in dealing with other people. The messages usually are quite clear, rooted in feelings and intuitive urges.

* * * * * * * * * *

You can readily discern which ego state is in control at any given time. There are four check points:

1. Observe your behavior. This can include your posture

– the way you sit, stand, and walk – and your voice – words you select, and intonations. Common words from the Parent are cute, marvelous, awful, childish, filthy. Child words might be gee, wow, won't, and can't. The Adult speaks up in terms of suitable, practical, logical, and correct.

2. Observe how you get along with other people. The Parent will take a run at being bossy, or take a know-it-all stance, often upsetting the Child in other persons. If your Child is fun-loving and happy, the Child in others will enjoy your company. When your Adult is in charge, chances are that the Adult will surface in persons with whom you interact.
3. Check your early years of childhood for clues. Do you remember how you spoke as a pre-schooler? How your parents talked? Sometimes you will catch yourself talking exactly the same as you did as a child. Other times you will hear your mother's or father's voice in your own.
4. Check your own feelings. This is the most important test. As Shakespeare put it, "To thine own self be true." You can actually feel your ego states at any given moment, and alter them to best suit the situation.

* * * * * * * * * *

The Child is probably the most important inner state. It never goes away. And you wouldn't want it to, because the Child is the most fun. It provides your play state. The Adult's job is to meet the Child's needs without getting into trouble. You want the Parent within to treat the Child with respect and love.

Ask yourself: How do I treat myself? What kind of Parent am I to myself? Do I have a scolding Parent, or an encouraging Parent? If your mother and/or father criticized more than encouraged, your internal Parent probably is more fault-finding than helpful. Similarly, if your parents did not openly display their love for you, your Parent within probably does not treat the Child within with love.

Contamination complicates the coexistence of the three ego states. Contamination results from influencing. The Parent and Child can interfere with the Adult and influence your feelings and actions. You might think you are operating from the Adult viewpoint, but if you are prejudicial the Parent probably is doing all the talking.

Example: If your mother believed that persons of another race or creed were inferior, your Adult voice might be contaminated by your Parent. The Adult might process your mother's influence as fact, without checking its validity.

The Child also can contaminate the Adult. If you have some paranoia, thinking people are against you when they actually are not, that is probably the Child in you running scared, and running over the Adult's thinking pattern.

Beware of getting in a rut, known as the "constant" state. That is when you allow one of the three ego states to remain in control too long and therefore at inappropriate times. The "constant" Parent, Child, or Adult operates at the expense of you developing into a whole human being. This is called exclusion – two of your ego states become excluded.

Once you become skilled at determining your own personality, style influences, and modes of operation, then you can use the same techniques to recognize the personalities and styles of persons you interact with.

All of it adds up as part of the continuing equation for better communicating, coping, and controlling your life events.

EXERCISE 9

Listed below are diagrams that can be used in your analyzation of personalities.

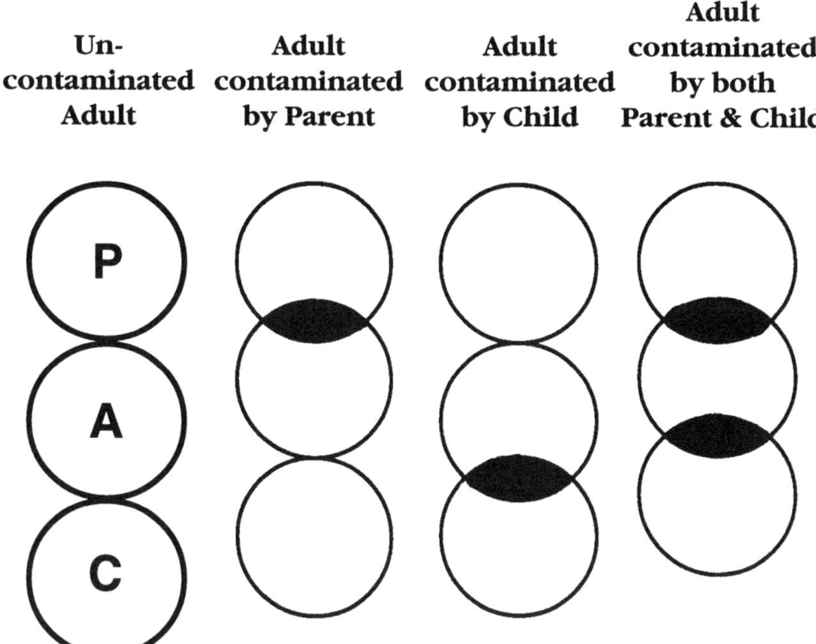

Once you have a feeling of your own personality, fill out an Ego Chart to graph your identified ego states. Next, ask some people who know you well to fill out an Ego Chart based on their perceptions of your personality. Carefully compare and evaluate these Ego Charts to determine the areas where you would like to make improvements. When these areas have been identified, begin the development of a plan to make the changes and proceed in doing just that!

EXERCISE 10

Ego Chart

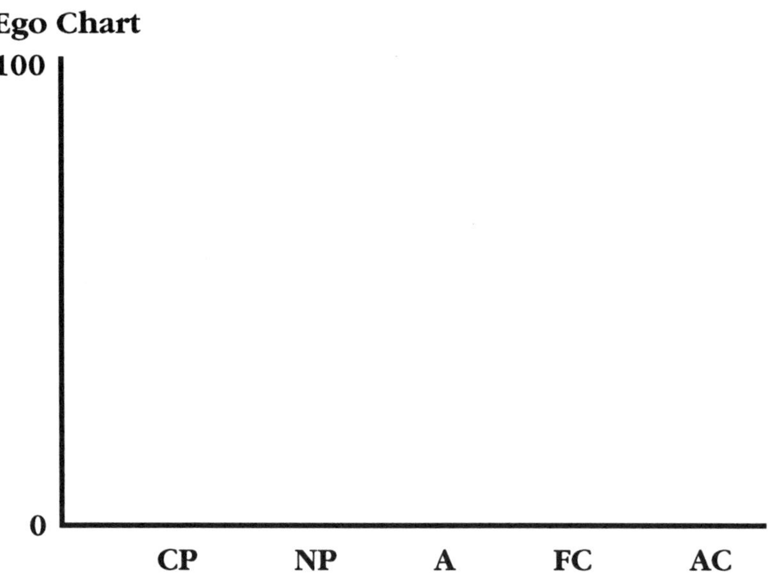

**Critical Parent (CP)* is that part of the personality which is critical and negative.

**Nurturing Parent (NP)* is that part of the personality which is nurturing and caring.

**Adult (A)* is that part of the personality which is objective and realistic.

**Free Child (FC)* is that part of the personality which is child-like and playful.

**Adapted Child (AC)* is that part of the personality which is able to adapt to positive and negative situations.

Conclusion:

1. Ego charts can be completed with all parts of the personality totaling 100 percent.
2. Ego charts can be completed with all parts of the personality exceeding 100 percent.
3. An ego chart can be used specifically to determine your own personality, as well as a tool for diagramming the personalities of persons you work with.
4. Use an ego chart to specifically identify the way you handle any given problem or situation. Look at the results and determine why you handled it the way you did, and changes you might make in future interactions.
5. No basic guideline suggests what percentage of your personality should comprise each ego state. You determine that based on how you feel about each facet of your personality, and the results you are getting. A person with strong self-esteem might do well going through life with 75 percent nurturing, loving Parent dominant. Another with the same degree of Parent in charge might develop an ulcer because of insecurities and feelings that others are taking advantage of him.

16

You Are Human, Too

The more things a man is ashamed of, the more respectable he is.

— *George Bernard Shaw*

Theme: You are human, too. Therefore, you are susceptible to mistakes ... no one has all the answers.

Empathy, as I have stated throughout my work, is instrumental in attaining success in human interaction. Especially in dealing with conflict, anger, and difficult persons and situations.

This underlying base of understanding means you can only expect others to be perfect when you yourself are perfect.

Thereby, others are on safe ground.

Avoid demanding from life all the time, and concentrate more on giving – at least a little bit...and eventually a lot. Do things for others. This provides simple access to a rich, full life.

The human condition is interesting in that experiences appear universal – across boundaries of rich, poor, tall, short, fat, skinny, light, dark, American, foreign. Events occur in different nuances and circumstances, and during different life cycles, yet they seem to occur with an overall sameness. Nobody is exempt from whatever experience or difficulty you can name.

All living persons experience joy and despair.

One of the most important and influential learning experiences is to embrace your human frailty, and to forgive yourself. A friend once told me, "Start the day looking in the mirror and saying, 'Today you will be the best person you can possibly be.' At night before sleeping, look in the same mirror and say, 'I forgive you for not making it.'"

The profound importance of this trait is that it paves the way for learning from all experiences. Each of us will make mistakes, and it behooves us then to develop the skills to learn from those erring ways, and minimize and deal with them in acceptable ways.

By viewing and accepting the commonality of humankind, we also eliminate prejudices that are chains forged by ignorance to keep people apart. We must never bypass an opportunity to assist any person because of some preconceived notion or bias.

* * * * * * * * * * *

A common and mostly misunderstood problem is mental depression. It has stalked some of the best and brightest throughout history – Abraham Lincoln, Queen Elizabeth I, Marilyn Monroe, Elvis Presley, and former Secretary of Defense James Forrestal, among those who made their illness public.

Countless millions suffer from depression to some degree, and a large percentage deal with severe states, such as manic depression that subjects its victims to bouts of despair and mania throughout most of their lives.

Alcohol addiction remains a constant problem in American society, and research suggests that nearly half of all alcoholics experience some form of depression. Men outnumber women in these findings, four to one.

Doctors have documented that depression occurs at an increasingly and alarming earlier age. Through the years depression commonly has been categorized as something that occurs in mid-life, ages 40-50. Now we are finding that the peak years for major depression disorders ranges from 25-44, with a significant decline after age 60.

About half of depressed persons become suicidal. We will come back to that later.

Depression involves specific symptoms ranging from sadness and grief to low self-esteem, irritability, hopelessness, disinterest in sex, sleep disorders, loss of appetite, decreased energy, difficulty concentrating, no involvement in hobbies, and suicidal tendencies.

Burn-out, either personal (emotional) or professional, or a combination of the two, is a major cause of depression. It is important to monitor your tendencies toward burnout.

The following exercise will help you determine your burn-out level. Answer the questions honestly and use the results to help plan your future course of action.

EXERCISE 11

Answer these questions with a rating scale of (1) absolutely no, (2) probably no, (3) sometimes, (4) probably yes, (5) absolutely yes.

___ Do you feel irreplaceable?
___ Do you dread weekends?
___ Do you feel powerless to make a difference in people's lives?
___ Do you feel persistent pressure – too much to do, too little time?
___ Do you wish you could spend more time doing what you want to?
___ Has your physical appearance changed for the worse?
___ Are you losing things more often?
___ Are you over-extended?
___ Do you feel like fighting with people frequently?
___ Do you feel unappreciated?
___ Are you arguing more with your spouse, children, friends?
___ Do you get depressed?
___ Do you feel nervous when you try to relax?
___ Do you have recurring colds, back pain, or insomnia?
___ Do you feel guilty over a lack of success as a human being?
___ TOTAL SCORE

Total score index:

15-30 You are doing excellent in coping with life and its problems.

31-39 You are doing fine, but pay attention to any changes in attitude, feelings or behavior.

40-49 You are on the edge of personal burnout. Take preventative action.

50-60 You are slipping into warning stages. Red lights are blinking.

61-69 You are sliding into an alarming burnout stage. Sirens are sounding.

70-75 You are burned out with life and failing to cope. Seek help at once.

* * * * * * * * * * *

Dedicated, caring people can avoid burnout by understanding themselves, by boosting self-confidence, and by accepting themselves as less than perfect. If perfection is your goal, you have set yourself up for automatic failure. (Who do you know that is perfect?) If excellence is your goal, you have set yourself up for all possibilities for attainment.

Recognizing negative stress and relieving it before it mounts is a way to avert burnout tendencies. Managing anger goes a long way, too. Other keys are managing priorities (commonly called time management), taking a healthy attitude about change (which is constant), and letting go of things out of your control.

* * * * * * * * * * *

One of society's most wasted resources is human potential. Everyone has potential. One of life's great tragedies is the person who, failing to realize her or his self-worth, commits suicide.

A quirky statistic is that the suicide rate has remained relatively constant over the last 30 years, upward to 100,000 a year, although the actual number is believed to exceed by three times the number that are reported.

As a parent and/or teacher, the most alarming trend is suicide among youths 15-24 – the third leading cause of death in the United States after homicide and accidents. Statistics on suicides by children ages 5-14 would sicken you.

Recognition skills for clues to suicidal tendencies are of the utmost importance, if we are to have a prayer of saving lives of "lost" young people.

Clues:

- Withdrawal from social contact, isolation, non-communication, loss of interest in school and activities, general apathetic attitude.
- Aggressive behavior – defiance, disobedience, rebellion.
- Overt statements such as, "I wish I were dead," or "You'd be better off without me around."
- A request for suicide prevention information for a friend or relative.
- Giving away possessions, getting affairs in order.
- Increase in drug or alcohol consumption, or abuse.
- Previous attempts at suicide.
- Disorientation.
- Over-eating, or loss of appetite, dramatic changes in weight.
- Sleep problems – either insomnia or excessive sleeping.
- No laughing or smiling or other outward signs of happiness.

- Slowdown in speaking pace, in walking, or in everyday activities.
- Increased preoccupation with internal conflicts.
- Apprehension, anxiety, tearfulness, or crying jags.
- Facial expressions that reflect no liveliness, slumping posture, no spring in the gait, lack of animated gestures.

Any of these that occur briefly, as isolated conditions, warrant no alarm. If a condition, or several together, persist over an extended period of time, take action. You are always better off to act when it turns out unnecessary (and risk looking a little foolish or protective) than to fail to react when intervention is needed (risking a life).

What is appropriate action to take? Guidelines:

- One of the first things to do is *something*. Even if it is awkward, some action is good, because hesitancy can prove fatal.
- Take any threat of suicide seriously. Youths most often confide in their peers, so alert them.
- Broach the subject yourself. Ask the person point-blank, "Are you thinking about killing yourself?" Some fear that direct mention of suicide invites trouble – plants the idea. Research does not support this. If danger signs persist, chances are the person already has actively considered suicide, and bringing it into the open can only help.
- Encourage the person to talk at length about whatever is bothering him or her. *Listen!* Listen without judging or criticizing or arguing. Suicide is a statement of low self-esteem, so say whatever you can that is encouraging.

- Legitimize the person's problems. They are big to that person, and demeaning or minimizing the problems is not warranted. The last thing this person wants to hear is that everything will be OK, because life can't be that bad. The suicidal person is convinced that life will always be bleak.
- Avoid any life vs. death arguments. Your goal is to appeal to the person's feelings of personal worth and dignity; insist on talking about life only.
- Seek professional help readily. Many people are afraid that visiting a psychiatrist, psychologist, or counselor makes them "crazy" in the eyes of others. Hesitancy to admit to emotional problems stems from the implication of being a failure or loser.

Each individual can be a lifeguard, and life saver – a one-person committee to prevent suicide. You need no elaborate pieces of equipment, no special technical knowledge. The only tools you need are right at hand – your eyes, intuition, a pinch of wisdom, alertness, and the ability to act and speak appropriately, with compassion and empathy and deep resolve.

17

The Golden Rule

Do unto others as you would have them do unto you.
— The Golden Rule

Theme: Above all, treat other people with the respect, kindness, compassion, understanding, and dignity that you would like to receive from them.

Most of us are quick to criticize when we observe someone else treating or talking about people disrespectfully. Low-grade, off-color remarks, a lack of concern for the welfare of others, and dehumanizing behavior all contribute to poor self-concepts. [The rich irony is that such behavior stems from low self-esteem and poor self-image in the person who is railing about the inadequacies or differences of other people. The only way the derogatory person can feel good is by putting other people down.]

Here are some questions to answer in gut-level honesty with yourself:

- As the controller of your life, are you putting strong

faith, love, confidence, effort, and Golden Rule into your day-to-day interactions?

- Are you guarding against negative thought patterns, dwelling on yesterday's mistakes or failures?
- Are you discoloring thoughts by expecting the worst (pessimism)?
- Are you harboring deeply-imbedded resentments?

You can change your life if you have too many undesirable answers to these questions, and if you so desire to change.

Positive growth begins immediately, when you are committed to it. You become what you think you are. For dramatic improvement in your daily living, try the following for the next 10 days:

1. Begin each morning by expecting the best to happen that day.
2. While dressing, shaving, or making breakfast, say aloud some positive affirmations. "This is going to be a wonderful day"…"I can successfully handle anything that happens today"…"I feel good mentally, physically, emotionally"…"It is great to be alive"…"I am thankful for all that I have had, all that I have now, and all that I shall have."
3. Throughout the day, deliberately speak hopefully about everything — your work, your health, your future, and other people.
4. Avoid arguments.
5. Whenever a negative attitude is expressed, counter it with a positive, optimistic opinion.

The famed poet Ralph Waldo Emerson said a mouthful when he wrote, "They who believe they can, conquer." Fill your mind with thoughts of faith, confidence, and security.

* * * * * * * * * * *

This final exercise will raise a host of issues that people must attempt to work through in a rational manner. The discussion usually provides a dramatic example of our value differences, the difficulty of objectively determining the best values, and the difficulty in applying the Golden Rule.

EXERCISE 12

Please note — this exercise is designed for group activity, but can be useful for individuals working alone to analyze their own reactions to the situation.

Divide into groups of 6-7 persons. Assume your group works in Washington, D.C., in a department in charge of experimental stations in far outposts of civilization. Suddenly WWIII breaks out and bombs start dropping. Places all across the world are being destroyed. People head to whatever fallout shelters they can locate. Your group receives a desperate call from one of your experimental stations, requesting help.

The station has 10 persons in it, but their only nearby fallout shelter contains enough space, air, food, and water to support just six persons for three months. They realize that if they decide among themselves which six will go to the shelter, they are likely to become irrational and start fighting. They have agreed to abide by the decision that your department makes in selecting the six.

You will choose with just a superficial description of the 10 persons, and you have just 30 minutes to decide before you have to leave for your own shelter.

Make the following considerations:

- The six persons you choose might be the only people left to start the human race up again after the war subsides.
- Disallow yourself to be swayed by pressure within your group. Choose wisely and swiftly, because if you fail to meet the 30-minute deadline you will leave the 10 to fight it out for themselves, with the possibility that more than four might perish.

Here is all you know about the 10 persons:

1. Bookkeeper, male, age 31
2. His wife, six months pregnant.
3. Black militant, second-year medical student
4. Famous historian, author, age 42
5. Hollywood actor or actress and singer
6. Biochemist
7. Rabbi, age 54
8. Olympic athlete, multi-sport star
9. College co-ed
10. Policeman with gun (they cannot be separated)

Discuss and choose. When the 30 minutes is up, each group shares its selection with the other groups. Observe the values implications that surfaced in the process.

How well did you listen to others in your group and value their opinions? Did you allow yourself to yield to pressure and change your mind? Were you (or anyone) so stubborn that the group couldn't make a decision? Did you feel you had the right choices? What do your selections say about your values?

[Let the participants decide whether these questions are written about privately, or discussed openly by the group(s).]

A hand-lettered poem was signed by several students and written by a 16-year-old who had been in detention for abusing her parents:

You've been our friend through good times and bad.
You've made us happy when we were feeling sad.
Well, now we're here to return the task,
All you need to do is ask.
We'll be waiting and praying for your arrival,
For if it weren't for you,
What would be the chances for our survival?

18

Letters from AEP Students

From a confidential letters file (with students' names changed, and grammar and spelling unedited) you can glean a sense of the breadth and depth of problems young people have created for themselves. I corresponded with them regularly, most while they were incarcerated.

As you peruse their thoughts and emotions, notice how they are reaching out, latching onto whatever ounce or two of caring and hope they can. These are not all success stories. Everything doesn't always come up roses. They did not all have happy endings.

The point isn't that all of a sudden life becomes tidy and wonderful for the down-and-out. But notice the strain throughout the correspondence of these kids wanting to do better. Can you hear them? The message remains steadfast and clear – without listening, without caring, without hopefulness in communication, you have naught but a silent killer.

Empathy over apathy, that is the message.

* * * * * * * * * *

[The first sequence of letters with a former student in the Alternative Education Program where I was principal blows me away. He wrote after we had implored the legal system to keep him in a juvenile program rather than the state prison system. His letters, and the staggering follow-up from a friend, serve as constant reminders to me of what we educators are up against, and of how we must remain vigilant and diligent in striving to reach these kids.]

Dr. J,

Hello sir, I just wanted to thank you for writing to the courts about me and telling them they should keep me in the juvenile court system. I really do appreciate it, even though they waved me to adult status. I was in the county jail for about 3 months, then placed in Department of Corrections. I was their for about two weeks.

They do a whole bunch of testing like academic, health, psychological, and then you do substance abuse testing, then once your done you see a counselor and they tell you your security level that you'll be on.

I am now serving a 51-month sentence, which is about 4 years and 3 months. They classified me minimum security so I kind of lucked out, being my crime was a level 2 security and a B felony and having two counts.

I just want to thank you and the teachers I had (at AEP) and the secretaries for being so good to me.

Sincerely,
Jeremy

(A few months later)

Dr. J.,

Thank you very much for writing. Sounds like your having a big year at school. Well so far in here I've completed a literacy program, witch touches you upon math and english. I have also gotten my G.E.D. already, too, the teachers said that I had some very high scores on my tests that I took.

I've got a job as a night porter, I work from 12 at night till 6 in the morning. We get paid 75 cents a day, the money that we earn goes on our accounts. Its not much, but its better than nothing at all.

Your right about all of the negative things that happen while being imprisoned I've seen a lot of it and experienced some of it too. Its very hard to avoid. Well I have to go for now.

Merry Christmas.
Jeremy

Another AEP student, in response to assignment following Christmas, wrote this next letter, which was unsigned and marked confidential.

I don't know what to write about, so I'm going to write about my friend Jeremy. As you know, he is dead.

Jeremy was my best friend. He told me everything and did everything with me. He was like a brother. I can't imagine life without him. But now I have to.

At his funeral I saw him and he looked alive. I kept thinking he would jump up out of the cascet. But he didn't. I didn't know just how many friends Jeremy had until I saw them at the funeral. I cried. All my friends cried.

Who I really feel sorry for was Tish, Jeremy's girl friend they gave her his hat and his shoes that he was wearing when he got shot. She won't take them off.

Jeremy and I used to go to good times and play pool every day and every night. We lifted waits together. Then we would go out and party all night long getting drunk and stoned. We were put on probation together. We were some crazy people I tell you.

We use to do some of the stupidest things a man could only dream about. Once me, Jeremy, CJ, and my dad went to the lake to camp. Jeremy stole the boat and got lost somewhere in the lake and we could not find hour way back untill we saw my dad driving around to find us.

I will never forget the time Jeremy, Jamie, my mother and I went to the renesonts (Renaissance) festival. We entered the food contest, where the cleanest turkey bone won. I came in first by a hair, Jeremy came in second barly. Jamie would have if he wouldn't of took so long. We had my mother beat by a mile. We were playing around with their sords. At the end my mother bought us all necklaces to remember the renoconts festival.

We played football a lot over by Jeremy's apartment complex. A cupal of times we went out and picked up some girls. He loved listening to music and watching TV, but what kid doesn't. He was very smart, but he did not want anyone to know. Well I know everything about him, because he told me.

Now he's dead.

* * * * * * * * * * *

[Jeremy had been shot to death in a gang-related confrontation.]

Dr. Jackard,

Hellow. How is AEP coming along? Did the school district change anything about what goes on in AEP? I hope not.

I don't think anyone except you and the staff could understand how much AEP means to me. For the longest while school was my only motivation for getting out of here (jail), but I realize that I probably won't make it.

I found a new motivation. It's for myself. I do hope to make it out for Field Day. I have only 4-1/2 weeks to go.

I will try to read a chapter from the Bible every day, and pray every night. Not only does he show me whats right, but gives me hope and shows me how lucky I really am to have the things I do.

Your doing good things. Keep it up.

See you later,
Student Rex

* * * * * * * * * * *

[The following is another sequence of letters from a young man who was biding his time in prison awaiting trial. He, too, had been a student at the AEP high school. We corresponded regularly.]

November

Dr. Jackard,

I got your letter yesterday and it was real good to hear from you, and how things are going at school. I heard that the police are looking for John, but I ain't for sure what they want him for.

I have learned a lot since I been here and know what I got to do to stay out of trouble so I can take care of my daughter. I've made some bad choices, but now I want to put all of that behind me and start all over once I get out.

There is a lot of people who don't understand that there real friends are their family and them are the only ones who are their for you when your locked up. I have learned the hard way and the only person I can blame is myself.But that's gonna change when I get out.

Thank you for all you have done for me. My brother sees the parole board early of December. I'm sure he'll get paroled and get his life together. I still hope you let me go and talk to people for you once I get out.

I go to jury trial Dec. 19th and it is suppose to last a week long. Hopefully I'll be home for Christmas. The D.A. wants to ask the judge if she can use my priors against me and some other stuff. I can't believe it has tooken me this long to have learned my lesson.

Caesar

The next February

Dr. Jackard,

I've been working on my case. I go to trial soon. I got a good chance at winning. I got enough evidence to show to the jury that it was self-defense. I sure can't wait until I get out. So I can get my life straight.

The streets was there when I was born, and are going to be there when I die. So once I get out I'll have business out on them. I got a beautiful daughter who needs a father, and I can't be know father in and out of jail.

I've learned so much here. A lot more people will be learning the hard way like I am. I wished society would help out kids when they're young and getting into trouble. I hope I can continue talking to people for you once I get out. I hope you enjoy my letter. Take care.

Caesar

p.s. write back when you've got time

March

Dr. Jackard,

I got a problem with two counselors at your school. I was talking to Anissa on the phone the other day, and me and Anissa haven't been getting along that well. So Anissa went to talk to (the counselors) about our problem. I was happy that she did so she would get it out of her instead of keeping it inside of her.

The problem is (the counselors) keep telling her not to wait for me, and that she should go on with her life. Now our problem has gotten even worse. Would you please tell (the counselors) how I feel about the stuff there telling Anissa.

Thank you,
Caesar

June

Dr. Jackard,

I got to go to bootcamp next month for 180 days. Then once I get done I'll be on probation for 36 months. I thought this plea bargain would be the best thing for me. If I would have went to trial and lost I would have to do 5 years in prison. I got a daughter and couldn't afford to take that chance.

I plan on going to junior college. Me and Anissa plan on getting married in a couple of years. Thank you for believing in me. I know I ain't going to hang around with people when I get out....just my family because they're the only ones who comes and sees me and puts money on my books.

We only live once on earth, and I want to spend that time with the people who love me. I know I ain't going to change over night, but I'm gonna stick at it. I want to stay on the rite track for the rest of my life, and not get into trouble anymore. It's to bad that I had to learn the hard way.

Sincerely,
Caesar

* * * * * * * * * * *

Hi. A lot has been going on lately. I have anorexia.

Well, I'm getting over it anyway. I have always dealt with my problems by myself. I've always been the type of person that other people tell all their problems to. My entire family have always done that to me and so do most people I've been in school with.

I always help other people out when they need it, but if it were the other way around, they wouldn't be there for me. I'm too quiet for my own good, I guess. I'm not shy, I just don't feel the need to speak up.

For everything that has happened to me, I blame myself. In the past, blaming myself has taken the form of self mutilation, isolation, and most recently, anorexia. No matter how hungry I was, I would not eat.

It all happened so fast. Sixty pounds in three months.

What I had wished for for so long was coming true ... death. Three weeks ago I was dying. Once you've spent so much time thinking about that and working yourself to the core, it's hard to let go of.

(unsigned)

* * * * * * * * * * *

Dear Mr. Charles Jackard,

Hi. I'm a former gang member. I read your article in the newspaper [about gang behavior] and liked it. Now all this worrying about, are the gang members going to come to an agreement on peace? Yes, they will for the simple fact that most of them have children and I'm pretty sure they don't want their children growing up in a gang like they did.

See I'm 20 years old and don't have children and I thank the Lord for that, because if I was a father I wouldn't want my child to be in my teenage shoes running around carrying guns and drugs on them.

Now when I joined the Crip gang I didn't join it just to kill people, which I never killed anyone, I joined to get respect and to make money and to have some things I never had such as a nice car and better clothing that's all.

Like you said in your article, "Most kids do not join gangs because they want to fight, break the law, or get into trouble." And that's true. Some join because they don't want to go to school, work, or take authority from people such as parents, teachers, or bosses and that's the category I fell under.

But now that I'm almost 21 it's time to be an adult and a role model for the younger generations and led them the right way. So the point is, I feel your article has helped me out and given me more encouragement to help other gang members.

Thank you,
Macie

p.s. If you would write back or come visit and talk to me, I would appreciate it.

* * * * * * * * * *

[These letters from a former student in jail came two months apart . . .]

November
Dear Dr. J.,

I was glad to hear from you. I'm doing fine, everything in here has been a real learning for me. I have to learn to be a mature person, and finally know what I got to do to be successful. I know once I am home I have to start over for Cindy, Andreya, and me.

I have kept in contact with Joan. I only wish that these kids who are causing such violence could see what they face. I told Joan to learn to be a successful person, and that it is nothing nice in here.

I'll see the parole board in 7 days and hopefully I'll be home. I'm going to work and go to a community college. I also want to help kids who are like me stay out of trouble.

Thank you for believing in me, and always standing by me. I'm going to make something of myself. I know that it will be hard, but I'm up for the challenge. My friends and family wait for me, write me, and we always talk on the phone.

Will you please ask John or Natalie to write. I have a few things I need to say to John. I'll visit the school once I'm home.

Alex

January

Dr. J.

I got good news 3 weeks ago. I'm going home (in two months). I know now what I found out...what it will take for me to be successful Doc. I have my act together. I plan on attending a community college and working.

I appreciate your support...(and) the impact it has had on my life. My brother is staying strong and trying to get through this mess. My heart goes out to John. I really thought he would learn to be a man, instead of a child. I wish I could get down and talk to him.

I wish that I would not have been hard headed, maybe I wouldn't have caused my family so much grief. I can say at least I learned from my mistakes. I will come by the school and help you with your talks to help kids like me before they reach the point where I'm at. My attitude has made a 100 degree turn.

So you had 20 graduates. AEP is a good school and I'm glad people are graduating instead of dropping out.

Sincerely,
Alex

* * * * * * * * * * *

Dr. J,

Funny how mysteriously time passes by, eh?

Don't notice the changes in myself so much as others. When visiting pals or long-lost cousins, my knees buckle at the stupendous growth and acceleration of pituitary gland responses, adolescent stubbles, frisbee-winging teens who've gone into rapid stages of growth and productivity. Makes me feel old, ya' know?

Have yet to notice any grey spots, still awaiting my first social security check, but am noting changes about me that fail to reassure me of my long-lost youth. Mile High victors are the local boys, and long gone are my diploma-seizing days of 1991. And my youth is sooo lost, ladies and gents.

As my age has bypassed my fake ID, I find it harder and harder to order a special kiddy plate and damned-straight impossible to gather the ol' bunch that was oh-so-damningly prepared for tackle football.

Am now a happy-go-lucky college student. Prepped for a report card showing a steady 3.0, I still find more than enough time to wander the local bars, and a helluva lot more time to reminisce everyone who helped me get through high school. Oh, and an irritbale James Cagney I was, huh?

...Graduated with honors, and rolled through my first year at college in a drugged-up, washing-out freeze, but have rallyed ever since, going full-fledged into journalistic maneuvers and broadcasting interests. Have yet to make that first million, but well on the way to making my old (AEP) school proud.

Drive by there every so often, and recollect my days

there NOT with jubilance and fondness, but more with pride and regret. Ever-hopeful that my life would one day return to normal, I left (AEP) proud of my maturation and accomplishments, but was quickly dispelled by both students and teachers who regarded my return to (regular) high school with doubt and ill-regard.

Have never told you all of my appreciation in helping me turn it all around, and I couldn't have done it without you. Thanks to all the faculty. You're worth so much, and impact so many.

Never forgotten,
David

* * * * * * * * * *

Dr. J,

I got your letter. I was surprised, but happy. I manage to keep myself under control. Since I been here I haven't lost control.

I have let a lot of God in me. He helps me out a lot. One thing that will be hard is stopping drugs. I wont totally, but I'll cut down on dosage.

Thank you. AEP means a lot to me...and helped me out so much. I think about it a lot. No matter what anyone says, it's a fantastic school. That's to bad about John and Caesar. I pray every night that people think before they do things, but not to stay clear of trouble; that is not happening.

When I get out I'll be back at AEP. Take care.

Rex

* * * * * * * * * *

Dr. Jackard,

I'm hanging in there. I've been here (juvenile detention center) about 10 months. This place can get real crazy. I'll get out soon if everything goes right. Natalie visits me every other weekend. I've been hearing a lot of stuff going on out there. I heard Alex went to prison 2-5 years. Jeeper got out of prison, Arturo is coming back from California, and Caesar shot some girl because she got in front of some dude he was shooting at.

I guess some people never learn. Every night I lay in bed my mind drifts over this 25 foot fence and wonder whats my girl doing and what would I be doing now if I didn't get caught. I would either be on the run or serving a life sentence for the murder of that kid and his friends.

I read my Bible in here every night and I know I've got a lot going for me when I get out. My thoughts have changed...I realize that not everybody is out to get you, so you don't have to be hostile to everybody.

My grandfather spent 26 years on death row and died there. My uncle killed two people and spent most of his life in prison. My other uncles all spent their lives in and out of prison. My cousin is on death row now. Even my father has been in and out. I want to break that chain. I want to be one of the first in my family not to go to prison.

Everybody out there wrapped up in that gang shit, they don't understand that it don't do nothing for you. Especially all those wanna-be's, they don't understand what's ahead of them. They think it's all a game. They'll end up on the short end. But they think they can handle it. Even the real ones (gang members) can't handle it when 5-6 dudes jump him in a bathroom with paddlelocks tied into a sock.

I pretty much stay out of trouble here. I get the respect I want. Nobody tries to punk me because they know I'm a stand up guy. Kids in here prey on the weak. If the weak have something they want, they take it. One day I was circled by a group of white kids who call themselves "The White Knights." They asked me to be in there click. I told them I'm here for a crime I committed and I came in by myself so I'm leaving by myself.

But us whites pretty much stick together in here. So do the blacks. I'm not joining any little YCAT gang. Nobody knows that I was in a gang except some who knew me outside. There's a lot of racial tension.

I'll make it out of here soon. I'm going to get my GED when I turn 16 because I heard I have no high school credits. If you ever need me to do another one of those talks I would love to, because I want to do everything I can to stop all of this bull shit!

(Signature whited out)

* * * * * * * * * * *

Dr. J.

I'm out of here in 10 days. I've been locked up damn near 8 months! Time just wasted away, 8 months down the tube! But this is my last time in anywhere. I'm only 15 and already spent over 2 years of my life in correctional facilities.

So what did you think of my home here? (Ha! Ha!) To bad you didn't see the real deal...staff threatening students, sometimes abusing them. They say when we're put here we lost our right against physical harm. They're allowed to use "the force needed to control us!" That's the bad thing. They take it too far.

I haven't had any problems here that I couldn't handle. I get the respect that I ask for. Man all I can think about is getting out of here. You know something I really miss? Carpet. I'm not kidding. Everything here is linoleum or concrete.

I got a job lined up at $6.50 an hour. It doesn't compare to the thousands I was making a week selling drugs, but it's legal. I was getting into some crazy stuff out there. Sometimes I wonder if God put me here to stop me from getting killed or killing somebody.

I got a lot to look forward to when I get out but life isn't going to be so damn hectic this time. I'm not going to have to carry a gun, or worry about getting shot in the back of the head without saying farewell to my family. Just dying. That's not how I want it to end. I want to die knowing I'm free from all the gangs and drugs and pennitentarys.

I've grown up quite a bit since I got locked up. I've realized hanging with a gang doesn't take no kind of heart, what takes heart is facing whatever you got to by yourself. Just put your back to the wall and keep your head up, show pride.

In here it's mainly 4 or 5 groups. There's the White Knight/Aryan brotherhood, a white gang of neo nazis who hate everybody. The nuestros familion (our family, in English), pretty much Mexicans. And there are the blacks. It's pretty easy to stay out of trouble if you keep to yourself...not much fighting. Everybody's trying to get out.

I'll call when I get out. I'd like to do some more of those talks for you. I got a lot to say! My mom asked me the other day if I have finally seen the light? I told her not yet, but I've seen way too much darkness!

(unsigned)

* * * * * * * * * * *

Dr. Jackard,

I am doin alright. I've talked with Lori a # of times, we're getting along a little better. My release papers came for the end of this month. It's a Sunday, so I will be coming to school the next day to enroll. Let me know how much money I need so my father doesn't have to take off work to come enroll me. I have a lot of plans when I get out, and new things to discuss in my speeches.

As far as Jason is concerned I really don't want much to do with him. He's been talking with Lori and beating her down cause she wouldn't let him keep his shot gun in her trunk. That's a punk, Doc. Anywayz I hope I am able to keep from clicking when I'm released.

The time here is getting to me and making me think kinda crazy. How is John doin, I hope good. I guess you were not able to do the favors I asked of you in the note I wrote a while back. If it's possible for you to get Lori some roses from me I will still be sure to pay you back.

Please let the teachers know I will be back soon. Please write back and answer as many questions as possible.

Love,
Joshua

* * * * * * * * * * * *

Dear Dr. J.

I just wanted to wright this letter to say one thing, Thank You.

Thank you for making me feel like I belong. From day one, everybody (at AEP) made me feel accepted. They liked me for who I was, not who I wanted to be.

Thank you for giving me a chance to succeed in life. If not for everyone at AEP I wouldn't have made it. You gave me hope, and made me realize I can do whatever I want if I put my mind to it.

Thank you for helping me through problems. If I needed someone to talk to I could come to your office or call you at home. I never needed to call your house, but I appreciated the thought that you would be there to listen to me and do whatever you could to help me.

Last but not least, thank you for just being you...a wonderful friend. If only there were more men out there like you, women wouldn't have to go through so much trouble to find a guy who cares. That's what I like most – you care about everyone.

Thanks Dr. J. (Big Dog).
Love,
Kim

* * * * * * * * * * *

[Letter decorated with hand-drawn holly and a heart...]

Dr. J, Teachers, and Staff –

Thanks to all of you for your help and support during my time of need. At A.E.P. I have matured a lot and learned a great deal about the real world and not the "Fairy Tale

Land" I though we all lived in.

I've been through an abortion, have had people harassing me, and I did a little harassing myself. Through it all you have been there to help me determan right from wrong.

I'm sorry to say this will be my last year with you. It is time for me to move on and prove to my old teachers, family members, and most important myself that I can succeed as long as I believe in myself and I use my abilities to their full potential.

Without you it wouldn't be possible! I promise I will make a good name out of A.E.P.

Happy Holidays,
Irene

* * * * * * * * * * *

Dear Dr. J,

A couple of reasons why I admire you:

1. You care about your students, kinda like they were all family.
2. You always try to reason with people and not just punish them.
3. Your personality – you never play favoritism and your always fair.

Thanks. Sincerely,
Crisi

* * * * * * * * * * *

[Letters from educators about a student...]

To Whom It May Concern:

On behalf of my student, Micah, age 15, for the past

year in the gifted education classroom (SEEK) at (a suburban public high school)...he has many gifts and talents...an interest in leaders who has studied sports legends and Civil War heroes.

He was excellent in group participation in the Young Men's Leadership Series...provided the artwork to greet the founder of the Stop Violence Coalition when she launched the Kindness Project at our school. In that project Micah was an appropriate leader, greeter, and participant.

He excelled in oral interpretation of poetry and as a sensitive and appreciative listener for a young poet in the classroom. His humor was delightful in an amazing interpretive reading from a book of humor ... developing a comedy routine for our lunchtime SEEK cabaret ... Micah's beginning in drama activities.

While I understand that Micah has made some serious and inappropriate choices, I pray that great care will be maintained to see that he is provided a strong situation where he has an opportunity to receive nurturing and daily structure. Micah expressed a desire to be placed at AEP. Dr. Jackard expressed a kind and supportive interest in working with him there.

Micah's father refused to sign the necessary papers to transfer him to AEP. I pray that in light of the circumstances that the placement may be reconsidered. I understand the serious nature of Micah's recent poor choice.

However, it is very dangerous for him to be placed in a situation where he has little or no supervision or chance to be nurtured. I trust that a recommendation is forthcoming that will be fully cognizant of Micah's great needs. He is a person of great gifts and potential. He clearly deserves the structure and nurturing to allow him to live.

Sincerely,
Gifted Education Facilitator

CC: Psychologist, counselor coordinator, social worker, gifted education coordinator, principal, associate principal, AEP principal.

* * * * * * * * * * *

To Whom It May Concern:

Working with Micah as part of the gifted program this year was a privilege. He has a broad knowledge in many diverse topics and a wonderful sense of humor. In a structured environment I found him to be a willing and motivated learner.

With great distress I learned of Micah's recent problem. I am very concerned about his well being and hope everyone involved in his case sees that he remains in a stimulating, well structured environment. He will be greatly missed in class!!

Sincerely,
Para-Professional SEEK Gifted Program

* * * * * * * * * * *

[This is a paper written by a beginning AEP student, age 15, who had been in three different behavior disorder programs in three years. The student led off with goals and issues, followed by a personal essay...]

FRONT PAGE

Alternative Ed programs should be more accessible – not dependent on bad behavior to get in.

Public Ed is not for everyone.

Trade schools.

More help for delinquent behavior.

Conformity – guidance survival skills for those who find it difficult to conform.

Designate classes that deal with issues rather than specific subjects.

Public Education definition:

You must climb up our stairs!!

What happens to the student who has no legs!!!

PAGES 2-3

I have not been doing good for a long time. I'm not sure why. I would really like to go to a school where I can do good and have help. I have talked to friends and teachers about this, and they suggested A.E.P. I want to go there and actually go a whole year without flunking.

They have counselors and classes I feel comfortable with. Classes are smaller so there is less chance to get into trouble. I know a lot of people in my school and every one of them expects me to get into trouble. I don't want trouble anymore.

My B.D. (??) class helps for 2 hours. What about the other 5 hours? I would miss my high school but at least I'll be passing. I know my dad doesn't want me to go to

A.E.P. but he isn't the one that is failing in everything. My whole family had trouble in school it seems. I don't know if it's my fault or not. I can't concentrate, listen, or cooperate within groups of people no matter how I try.

I wish that me and my dad and my brother could be more of a family. We have always been pretty good friends yet we have never really been a family. My brother is too busy with his friends and girls to be with me. My dad has other problems of his own, so I'm left to deal with my own problems and take care of them myself.

Most kids have a lot of people they can talk to. I only have my dad, my brother, and my friends. I feel more comfortable talking to my friends than my dad or brother. My dad and I hardly ever talk about anything other than sports or TV or something like that. I think all those things added up are what makes me get into trouble.

I just got something wrong with me.

If just want to do good, and going to A.E.P. will help, then I want to go to A.E.P.

[name whited out]

"If I can stop one Heart from breaking
I shall not live in vain;
If I can ease one Life the Aching
Or cool one Pain
Or help one fainting Robin
Unto his Nest again,
I shall not live in Vain."

—*Emily Dickinson*

19

Letters from Parents/Teachers

The results are clear-cut. A compilation of letters and case studies from my years as principal of the Alternative Education Program in the Shawnee Mission, Kan., School District gives you insight into the method and accomplishments resulting from the theories you have read about.

And one distinct, gloomy example reminds us starkly of the challenges, and why a revolution is so necessary. It reminds us not only of the futility so rampant among at-risk students of every kind (this one was gifted, not a juvenile delinquent), but also among parents and teachers.

Also, a few letters from teachers who have attended my graduate studies courses reflect the immediate impact of the methods on the outlook of teachers. A positive approach breeds optimism and renewed enthusiasm for the task at hand.

These are not intended to toot our horn (but why not!) ... rather, you can glean insight and encouragement from the experiences of real people – real parents with real children with real problems.

The letters and stories are edited for space considerations. You will see clearly how the methods and mission of the staff, wrapped in the loving, caring, empathetic approach to education that we all believed so strongly in at AEP, produced positive outcomes.

The last letter is stunning, cutting directly to the heart of our matters. It stings, as a solemn reminder of why our commitment must be steadfast.

Take heart. You can, and will, make a difference.

* * * * * * * * * * *

Dr. Jackard,

Last night our family experienced something that quite frankly we never thought we would: we watched our daughter Kim graduate from high school.

She has struggled with school her entire life. Her teachers always said, "She is a bright student with a million-dollar personality. She scores well on aptitude tests and is fully capable of making good grades." But she didn't; she didn't care about her education.

Along the way teachers suggested rewarding her, withholding privileges, getting counseling, special tutoring, helping her with homework, letting her do homework on her own — the suggestions were endless. We tried them all.

We held her back. We sent her to learning centers and counselors. We hired tutors. Everything. The result was always the same: short-term improvement, nothing permanent. She never missed class, she simply didn't perform the work and her grades fell steadily.

She never got into drugs, abided by all our rules at home, and never had trouble with the law. She is a nice kid!

When she brought home all F's during her junior year of high school, we held no hope that she could get out of the deep hole she had dug for herself. We were desperate.

As a last resort, we contacted you at the Alternative Education Program. After meeting with her counselor and principal, you gave us a tour of the school. To be very honest, we were apprehensive.

We had heard many things from different people about AEP – some good, some bad. But after walking through the halls and finding virtually all of the students and faculty genuinely showing respect for one another, we felt reassured. The students seemed to truly enjoy learning.

This was our last hope for our daughter's future. She started class the next day. We saw a change in her almost immediately. In the first few weeks, her grades improved and she actually enjoyed school. Successes came in small doses at first, then increased in frequency and size. She felt good about herself again. And about others.

During her three semesters at AEP she has become a beautiful young woman, secure with herself and confident she can achieve any goal. She enrolled at the local junior college with a plan to transfer to a four-year school. She always has had a love of music and children and wanted to be an elementary school music teacher.

We have no doubt that because of the help from the faculty at AEP that our daughter will become a happy, caring elementary school music teacher who will reach out to some child struggling just like she was.

All students have the right to become happy successful students. For whatever reason, they all do not succeed in the traditional education environment. Thank you, AEP, for without you, last night would never have happened and our daughter might never have achieved her dreams.

John and Barbara Parks

* * * * * * * * * * *

Dr. Jackard,

Thank you for the caring, learning, and fun environment you have provided for Kristina. The difference in her demeanor, attitude, outlook, and especially grades is phenomenal.

At the time we enrolled her at AEP I felt at a loss as to how to handle the seemingly downward trend she was experiencing in all areas. After hearing AEP's mission and goals and touring the school with a student who obviously was another of your success stories, I saw light at the end of the tunnel.

After meeting all of Kristina's teachers I understand why so many kids have been helped through the most difficult years of their lives. Each had nothing but positive things to say about Kristina and her progress, and you and they obviously care about the kids.

It is so refreshing to hear your child talk about what she did and learned in school in an upbeat, interested manner, and not complain about the teachers and their methods. Whatever you all are doing, it is 100 percent right!

Thank you for being there when we needed you.

Sincerely,
Kristina Panos

* * * * * * * * * * *

Dr. Jackard,

Our daughter Julee has been able to focus on her goals since she started at AEP this semester. We feel true joy seeing a teen look forward to getting up in the morning in eager anticipation of school! She has not shown this enthusiasm about school for quite a few years.

Our younger daughter Jenny, starting her second year of high school, feels very discouraged about dealing with some other students at school. She enjoys her classes, and she started the first couple of weeks hopeful and enthusiastic. Now, she is sad and angry, and doesn't want to be there.

She comes home with tears in her eyes too often. She is happy with all the teachers and has some nice, supportive friends, but sometimes a 15-year-old has trouble seeing positive things while feeling pain from negative events.

We have lived in the Kansas City area only one year, and Jenny is the kind of kid who bends over backward to get along with people. But she will not put up with being treated badly. She finds it difficult to come from another state and be accepted among many groups of kids.

Julee and Jenny helped each other through last year, which was very tough for both of them. Jenny wants very much to be a good student. She always has tried hard and has good goals.

She wants to attend AEP with Julee. It would be good for her to be with her sister. Julee says that the students there are all concerned about their future and tend to be more supportive and respectful of fellow classmates than the (traditional) high school was.

Please put Jenny on your waiting list to start as soon as possible.

Thank you!
Chris Jasper

* * * * * * * * * * *

Dr. Jackard,

We teachers at Colony Middle School are moving ahead with plans to implement the vast knowledge we accumulated from your class. We have completely overhauled our student handbook during our class meeting time.

This would not have happened without the impetus of your class. Our staff is very happy and totally supportive of the new handbook. They feel it will have a significant impact on the environment and atmosphere at school ... moving toward a positive, safe school.

One of the major issues is gang dress. We see a direct correlation between discipline problems and gang attire. We developed a letter stating our concerns, and the consequences of students wearing gang attire.

We generated a list from teachers and discipline files to identify our target group. We brought those students and their parents into a meeting. The students and parents who did not attend received the letter by certified mail. We involved students in the meeting because we felt they had a significant role in taking responsibility for their actions.

Many students challenged the letter as an invasion of

their first amendment rights. We stuck by the belief that it is not a first amendment violation if it directly affects safety in our school. We expect to be challenged in court, and we believe the courts will back us.

We have total support from the school district, so we feel pretty good.

Sincerely,
John Jay Miller, Lisa Morger-Miller,
Mike Vrvilo, Lisa Vrvilo

* * * * * * * * * * *

Dr. Jackard,

I can't tell you how much I enjoyed this class. It is absolutely the best education class I have ever taken. This is a must for any and all educators. I personally think it should be a requirement for all future educators.

I have learned invaluable information that I have already shared with numerous educators and few future educators. I just wanted to thank you and to compliment you on a great class.

I hope to get a chance this spring to make a trip up to your school and see it in action. That, too, I am sure will be a tremendous learning experience.

I am planning on taking another of these video classes next semester, but I am not sure which one at this time. Could you please send me a course syllabus for each of the other three video classes. If any are as educational as the Violence in Our Schools and Communities, it will be greatly appreciated.

Thank you again for the opportunity to have one of

the greatest educational experiences of my professional career by taking this class.

Dennis Darting
Director of Guidance, Paola High School

* * * * * * * * * * *

Dear Dr. J,

This has been one of the most emotional and moving classes I have taken. It has had an impact on my life because it has helped me to see another person's "reality" that I had never considered before. I am sure this will be beneficial to me as a teacher because I work with students who come from rough neighborhoods. I will now see them through different eyes. I have learned a lot.

Jon was a very moving speaker. His story is powerful and I think he could be beneficial in changing many students' thinking. I have talked with our DARE officer, Officer Haden, and she would like to have him come to talk with our DARE classes this school year. She is also in charge of Youth Cadets. She would like him to share with them also. Please let me know some possible dates and what I need to do to make arrangements. I also need to know the cost. If possible, we would like both of you to come.

Since taking this class, things I have learned have been on my mind constantly. Actually, it has been depressing because there is no "happy ending" or easy solution. I wanted to share something I learned in church last Sunday that is relevant to our class. I want to share it with you because it gave me some hope. Our pastor told us about the movie, "The Dirty Dozen." He compared this movie with Jesus' choice of his 12 disciples. Jesus did not choose straight A students to be his disciples. He did not choose what society considers "the best." He chose fishermen, tax collectors, betrayers, common people. This shows Jesus' nature. He saw in these sinners potential. He saw in them the potential to do incredible things. He knew their past experiences and used these experiences to help them teach others. Jesus used encouragement, leadership and teamwork, to help the disciples change. They had a positive impact on many people's lives.

Now I realize that we do not have Jesus' insight. However, we do have the ability to encourage others and look for the "gift" or talent each person is born with. This gave me hope. No matter how difficult or "bad" a student may be, we need to look for that special skill they have and encourage them to seek their potential.

Please find enclosed the papers I needed to do for these two classes. If I need to do anything else, please let me know. I want to thank you for offering this class. It really had an impact on my life.

Tami Ensor

* * * * * * * * * * *

Dr. J,

I hope you will accept this letter as a reflection paper. If not, let me know and I'll write one for you. I think what I have to say here is more important than a "reflection."

I have learned so much in the past few weeks attending your classes. As a teacher in an "at risk" school, the underlying factors are the foundation for failure for these children. I think that learning about the cultural differences and their input is so important to understanding the whole child. The effects of society, the sex, the violence, and the drugs that permeate into students' lives must be addressed and understood to be effective. In *Maslow's Hierarchy* it is stated that unless a child's basic needs, food, shelter, and love, are met, they are unable to perform in school, let alone succeed. Too many educators feel that since they are helpless to change a child's home life then just maybe if they ignore it those issues will not be a problem. How truly wrong and sad that is. I used to be that kind of teacher. My philosophy was that if we just act like we have "normal" lives, then we will learn like "normal" kids. It saddens me to think of how many kids I could have helped.

I think our district, and most districts in general, share this philosophy. They believe that a new coat of paint, some really cool playground equipment, and a few well-placed computers will make up for the shortcomings that so many children come to school with. It has become very obvious to me that the people who make the rules and spend the money are more concerned with the aesthetics that our schools send out to the public than with what really needs to be happening. The schools and programs that I was able to see the past few weeks did not put a band-aid on the "cancer" that eats always at our children's well-being and self-esteem. The successful schools put their funding, although limited at times, where it would do the most benefit, on the kids!

In the past few weeks I have not learned any new

cooperative learning strategies, nor have I learned any of the finer points of effective instruction, I already know a lot about those topics. I have, however, grown as an individual as a parent, and most of all, as a teacher. I can honestly tell you that no child will leave my classroom without me knowing about their life and doing what I can to enhance it or help them to overcome it. I feel that the past few weeks have enlightened me more as a person than any other time in my teaching career. Thank you, Dr. J, for showing me that reaching children takes more than teaching strategies and education hoopla. It takes heart.

Marcia Sprigg

* * * * * * * * * *

Dear Dr. Jackard,

I would be remiss if I did not take this occasion, in my last set of papers I will ever have to mail to you, to thank you for the opportunities you offered to me with your classes. I feel fortunate to have met you and been a part of the family of educators that *choose* to take your classes. I truly learned many things and know that I now have met the most empathetic human being in the world, you. I admire that quality in you and describe you to all my colleagues with that quality first and foremost.

Thanks, too, for the graduation ceremony, certificate and candy bar you provided on the last day of class. It was so rewarding to finish my hours and to be acknowledged for it in front of all of my classmates!

I would like to know if I can still come to your classes and audit them. I am interested in the subject matter and would like to stay abreast of topics without the hassle of paying and getting the grade. Would this be a possibility? I know there are others who are interested in this, too. I can pass on your answer to them also. Of course, I understand the need to allow the paying customer to be first, but I would like to have the opportunity to learn more and appreciate your thoughts on the matter.

Again, thanks for all you have brought to Columbia. You have made learning an easier task for many of us.

Joyce A. Coats

* * * * * * * * *

Dear Dr. Jackard,

I would like to thank you for teaching in Columbia. Being in your classes was a wonderful opportunity for me.

When I took my first class in the summer of '98, the guest speaker brought in guns and ammo in cases commonly carried by students. The presentation definitely made an impression. Every class I took had memorable elements like that. The articles, videos and speakers combined to make each class a pleasure and a learning experience.

The area I learned the most was compassion and empathy. After reading, listening to others' experiences (especially John's), visiting criminal facilities, and watching videos, I truly saw a side of life very different from my own. Your classes made me realize that the most important thing I can impart to my students is that I care. Thank you again for making me realize that nurturing and caring is my first priority.

Sandy Kinkead

* * * * * * * * * * *

Dr. Jackard,

This class has given me more tools and ideas to use with students in the urban schools where I teach in Kansas City, Mo. Positive self-esteem is extremely important to be successful (as a teacher) and a good role model for students.

Most of the students I teach do not have a positive role model in their lives. I never dreamed that I would be teaching in an inner-city school when I completed my education. I live in Johnson County (suburbs) and could not obtain a position in its district. When I was accepted in Kansas City, little did I know of the adjustments I would have to make with my teaching style.

I just completed my third year at this middle school. I did not think I would return after the first year, but I had a wonderful principal who encouraged and supported me. She said that the first year would be the hardest and each year after that would get better. Was she ever right.

Bingham (school) had a great reputation many years ago and the fell into deep trouble, with the students taking over, more or less, from what I've been told. Our principal turned it all around, and we are on the way to being a great school again. She uses ... the style and humor that your classes employ.

Keep it up.

Diane L. Johnson

* * * * * * * * * * *

And, finally, the shocker ... written as "an open letter from Mark's mother, Cindy Huston, 9-9-95...."

Opening Doors

To anyone who will listen:

Two weeks ago Monday I lost my son. My creative, intelligent, handsome boy sunk into a severe depression from which he saw only one way out. Sleepless and sad, he went into the park behind our house, wrote us a note telling of his love for us, and hung himself with his belt.

I never would have believed this was possible, and our lives will never be the same.

I am a teacher. I wanted to be a mother my whole life, and I didn't take the responsibility lightly. You name a book about children, self-esteem, etc., I probably read it and applied it. I knew Mark was going through a rough time since about age 13-1/2, and we tried to help him.

He had a new psychologist with whom he was building a very close relationship. We spent a lot of time together, listening and talking. He knew how much he was loved, and that the love we gave him was not contingent on his behavior. We would have done anything to help him.

Now it is too late.

Mark, like many gifted children, was a perfectionist. He saw the world in black and white. He got into trouble cutting class. Events spiraled tragically, and in his eyes he had permanently messed up his life. We find it ironic as parents that events that started with cutting class (how many of us have cut class in our lives?) built up to such a feeling of panic. Mark was very fragile emotionally when this happened, and his spirit simply couldn't handle the feelings of hopelessness in a world which he saw as corrupt.

We do not meet the needs of our gifted children. They

are so smart, we think, that they can take care of themselves. Many become depressed during the turmoil of adolescence because they see all the imperfections of the world around them – racism, corruption, hatred, selfishness – before they are strong enough to deal with them emotionally.

What a normal person sees with some perspective at age 20-25, Mark saw at 13. It ate away at him. His mind was too advanced, and his heart too big.

Intellect in school can often become a burden. Teachers feel pressure to teach the curriculum, and overlook students with different needs. Mark loved school through about the third grade. He saw teachers as people who loved him and helped him soak up as much knowledge into his little brain as he could. It was a safe place.

In the fourth grade, the mold became more defined. He felt he wasn't learning as much and that he had to spend time practicing things he knew long ago. He wasn't learning as much, so how does he explain this to himself? By thinking, "I'm not as smart as I was. I'm losing my talents."

The gifted resource teachers in our district were wonderful. Mark saw them as allies, and their rooms were a safe place. Unfortunately, they had no power. Little by little he began to distrust authority.

No one teacher caused my son to take his own life. But the world is a harsh, scary place to a sensitive boy, and school should have been a place for him to get away from the injustices he saw. He didn't need a tutor. He just needed to explore new things and keep learning. He found doors closed, because of inconvenience, or because things just weren't done that way. I went to school and fought for him many times, but those were battles I should not have had to fight. He could have given so much to the world, and now we all are the losers.

If Mark's talents had involved a football or running shoes, he would have had support everywhere he turned. We cannot control society's warped values, but our schools must seriously look at how we treat our gifted children. They must survive because of the support system, rather than in spite of it. Teachers would never say, "I don't want those slow learners in my room." But we are supposed to all understand if the gifted kids are not wanted because "they think the rules do not apply to them."

Mark was not a miserable child. He had big plans for the future. We had many happy times as a family. We shared much joy and laughter. Mark was a true friend, and he tried to make up for the injustices he saw by spreading his gift of humor. He touched the lives of many little children, teens, and adults.

We cannot lose anyone else. We must help gifted children feel their gifts are not burdens. Doors must be opened to opportunity. We owe it to Mark and others like him to fix the system — reach out our hands to help, and think about what the gifted child is going through in his private emotional turmoil.

A Final Example

One lovely Wednesday morning before classes began, my student teacher shared some alarming news. The night before at rehearsal for our all-school musical, a student told her that she and others were being threatened by another student.

I found the student who reported the incident, and she added other names to the complaint. After locating each student and getting their stories, I went to the dean of students. After hearing the complaints, the school police officer was called in. Each student was brought in alone and asked to recount what had happened to them directly with the accused. After all four students had shared their perspective, the accused was brought in.

The overall complaints from the students were as follows:

1. The accused would get into the girls' personal spaces, call them a bitch and said, "I'm gonna f-----g kill you!"
2. He constantly used severe profanity and threatening comments — only to often follow up with "just kidding."
3. To two of the students, he told them he would kill all of them on April 20 (Columbine and Hitler's birthday).

The four students reporting the incident did so reluctantly — for they are kind and compassionate students AND students rarely rat on each other. Because of the consistency in complaints and the reputation of the four — the accused was suspended for two days with two weeks of in-building detention. In addition, I made the decision that he would be pulled from the musical. The last consequence was too much for the student and his father.

I met with the student, his father, the dean and our school safety director. The father felt that his son had been ambushed. He felt that the students accusing his son had misinterpreted what his son had done and said.

He felt that his son should have been able to meet his accusers. Also, he was adamant that his son was NOT a red-flag kid.

After the father had his say — we shared our stance on the situation. I found that I was doing most of the talking, for I felt very prepared because of all of the Jackard classes I have attended.

I told the father that the students who reported the problems were great kids who were not malicious. I also pointed out that the student and father acknowledged his propensity for profanity — therefore there should be consequences. I disagreed with the father concerning having his son meet the accusers. You do not force victims to meet with their predator. Finally, I shared with the father that his son WAS a red flag. I felt that his son needed counseling — especially with anger-management. I also felt that the father needed counseling to become better in tune to what his son was really doing and feeling.

The father left with tears in his eyes, and I was totally undone. I had to go to my office and lock myself in with a box of tissues. I cried over the father's grief, the lost boy, the fact that neither really understood the serious nature of the boy's psyche, and finally, the simple fact that the boy would always hate me.

Yet, I would do it all the same — for I know it was the right thing to do.

Jennifer-Black Cone
Rock Bridge High School, Columbia, Missouri

Appendix I

The Vocabulary of Empathy

1. **empathy** – Understanding that is so intimate that a person readily comprehends the feelings, thoughts, and motives conveyed by another person. *[It is hard to have empathy, or relate to a person when you are angry with them.]*
2. **understanding** – Compassion and/or sympathy. *[Understanding the real needs of another person is part of being emphathetic.]*
3. **altruism** – Selfless concern for the welfare of others. *[Today's youths need altruistic persons in their lives.]*
4. **thoughtfulness** – Consideration. *[A little thoughtfulness goes a long way.]*
5. **experience** – An event or circumstances that a person has lived through. *[Troublesome experiences help us relate to the troubles that others experience.]*
6. **connection** – 1) Union; junction. 2) A bond; link. 3) An association of relation. *[Sometimes hearing the kind voice of another person forms just the connection needed to get through a hard time.]*
7. **unselfish** – Generous. *[One unselfish act of kindness is worth more than anything money can buy.]*

8. **listening** – 1) An application to hearing for content. 2) Paying attention. *[Reflective listening is the best kind.]*
9. **respond** – 1) To reply, answer. 2) To act in return. 3) To react positively or cooperatively. *[Instead of reacting judgmentally, we ought to respond empathetically.]*
10. **respect** – 1) To feel or show esteem for. 2) To show consideration for. 3) To relate or refer to; concern. *[We do not have to agree with someone in order to demonstrate respect for them as a fellow human being.]*
11. **faith** – 1) Confident belief. 2) Loyalty; allegiance. *[Having faith in another person is a risk without a mutually empathetic relationship established.]*
12. **trust** – 1) Firm reliance; confident belief; faith. 2) The condition and resulting obligation of having confidence placed in a person or belief. 3) Custody, or care. 4) Reliance on something in the future; hope. Trust also can be an verb. *[Trust is earned over time.]*
13. **peace** – 1) Absence of war or other hostility. 2) An agreement to end hostility. 3) Freedom from quarrels and disagreement. 4) Public security. 5) Calm; serenity. *[Peace is a state to strive for in our everyday lives.]*
14. **feelings** – Any affective state or disposition. *[Sensitivity to people's feelings is a good quality.]*
15. **affirming** – Declaring or maintaining something to be true. *[Honest acts of empathy can be life affirming.]*
16. **together** – In harmony, accord, or cooperation. *[When people work together, empathy is essential.]*
17. **unity** – Singleness of purpose or action; continuity. *[Having empathy can promote a sense of unity within a group.]*
18. **harmony** – Agreement or accord, as of feelings. *[Empathy facilitates harmony.]*
19. **affective** – Dealing with the emotional or cognitive

rather than with the tangible. *[Empathy is an affective concept.]*

20. **sensitive** – Susceptible to the feelings of others. *[To reflect empathy for another person requires sensitivity to their feelings and experiences.]*

Appendix II

People Are People: Part A

The following edited excerpts come from a 40-page booklet that Dr. Jackard wrote in 1978, which he led off with the statement, "I dedicate this work to all those people who have helped me learn about people — by clarifying my feelings and thoughts and by helping me to understand that basically people are the same. People are people."

The concepts are timeless in their application and usefulness as we deal with ourselves, and with one another, day to day, face to face. Dr. Jackard addresses both simple and complex psychological behaviors in a roll-up-your-sleeves and get-to-work manner. The work promotes better understanding of self and others. Some of the material has been expanded and massaged as a result of experiences over the more than two decades since the original publication.

Some are random observations — food for thought, as they say; some are inspirational readings or sayings, some are definitive methods for directing thought and behavior. They are presented in no particular flow.

Several thousand copies of this compendium have circulated through Dr. Jackard's students and workshop participants, and put to use by parents and administrators across the country.

The result: better human relationships. Who could ask for more?

* * * * * * * * * *

Learn to look at yourself in relationship to others. Put the theories into immediate practice. The principles apply to children, adolescents, and adults of any background because they share one thing in common — they all have feelings.

* * * * * * * * * *

Life is wonderful. When you experience life fully, you gain a sense of worth. You take on the full essence of what it means to be human. And once you become a full human being, you'll never settle for less.

Joy is wonderful. When you experience joy, you feel like running through the streets, singing and dancing. You don't need something to happen or someone else to create joy. It comes from within. Rejoice in living. Once you have known the joy of life, you'll never settle for less.

But when you experience pain and despair, allow yourself to feel those emotions fully, too. They are an integral part of life. To deny them is to deny humanness. Learn to experience pain. Allow yourself to cry, to suffer. To live without pain is nonsense.

Despair can be a marvelous teacher. If you have been hungry, you know hunger, you don't just imagine it. If you have been lonely, you know loneliness, it's not just something from a romance novel. If you have grown up in poverty, the knowledge of it stays with you forever.

Use your knowledge, good and bad, first to understand your human condition and then to grow from it. Ultimately, it will help you to rise above the pain and sorrow to joyful living, despite human frailty, and then to help you relate to others in similar circumstances.

That is the empathy that we have talked about throughout this book, spread with a healthy dose of non-judgmental, unconditional love.

* * * * * * * * * * *

People are people, but many prevailing myths get in the way of accepting all people as they are. Positions and titles, social status, racial slurs and other means of labeling people make me ill.

No person is better or worse than you or me. All people cry. All experience loneliness. All are confused. All experience the same problems that you and I experience. Recognize that, and you are looking life squarely in the eye.

Recognize that, and the door is open to free and honest and productive communication.

* * * * * * * * * * *

The worst loss in the world is the loss of human potential. *Everyone* has potential. The worst tragedy I have experienced in my work through the years is the discovery that a young person has reached the state of mind to consider taking his or her own life.

What good does it do to raise and educate and love our children if we lose them because they decide they are not worthwhile human beings?

* * * * * * * * * * *

THINGS YOU DIDN'T DO

Remember the day I borrowed your brand new car and dented it? I thought you would kill me ... but you didn't.

Remember the time I dragged you to the beach and you said it would rain, and it did? I thought you would say, "I told you so." But you didn't.

Remember the time I flirted to make you jealous, and you were? I thought you would leave me ... but you didn't.

Remember when I spilled pie all over your car seat? I thought you would smack me ... but you didn't.

There have been many things you didn't do when I was human. You put up with me, protected me, loved me.

And there were lots of things I wanted to make up to you when you returned from Vietnam ... but you didn't.

* * * * * * * * * * *

Seek understanding of others. Reread the quote in the beginning of this book from "Please Understand Me." Make it your credo.

Only demand that others be perfect when you become perfect. That makes them safe from your wrath.

Stop demanding life, and give life. Do things for people. Start with a little, move toward a lot. Give instead of trying to get.

This is a simple key to a rich, abundant life.

* * * * * * * * * *

I've noticed a tendency of people, especially young people, to think that others haven't experienced certain aspects of living, and therefore, how can they possibly understand? All of us experience the same things, the same problems. Maybe they come in different shapes and forms and clothing. Certainly they come in different life cycles.

But they come. Count on it. Nobody gets a free pass in this life. There are no exemptions. The wealthy and poor, the tall and short, the skinny and me ... uh, portly, the light and dark — we all get strong dosages of similar ups and downs.

Therefore, it is paramount to embrace yourself, to feed off the ups and forgive yourself for being human during the downs. Above all, gain from every experience.

That will open the path to full application of the Golden Rule. You will learn to look at individuals as fully human, like you, and not ignore or avoid or not even see another person because of a bias or prejudice.

Prejudices are chains forged by ignorance that keep people apart.

* * * * * * * * * * *

The only reality is now. Caring is now. Empathy is now. Live for now.

* * * * * * * * * * *

Life is not a destination, it's a trip. Life is not where you are going; it is the getting there. Let life happen in full, without fear. Life is beautiful. And full of surprises, if you approach it with no preconceived notions.

* * * * * * * * * * *

We do not remember days. We remember moments.

— *Cesare Pavese*

Appendix III

People Are People: Part B

Learn to identify various problems that *all* persons experience. This reinforces the basic premise that humanness is universal; none of us escapes it, in all its imperfection. The amazing part as we examine common problems is how like experiences keep cropping up.

Anyone who accepts that he or she is — as one well-known book title says — fully human and fully alive will find stimulation in examining the commonalities we share.

Anyone who is not human can stop reading now!

* * * * * * * * * * *

What are people like? Mostly, just like you and me. Same wants, same needs, same desires. Same wishes, same dreams, same realities — sometimes harsh. Same sensitiveness, same need for a response with the famous TLC.

Yes, Tender Loving Care drives the bus. When it does not ... well, the statistics show a stark result.

Some research suggests that at any given moment more people reside in facilities for treatment of mental illness than for all other diseases combined, including heart disease, cancer, and alcohol/drug addiction.

Alarming numbers among us have enough mild to severe emotional or mental disability to require treatment. Whether we want to admit it or not, most of us could benefit from group or individual counseling.

Prevailing symptoms and problems let us know how imperfect we are. The mind does not always function at 100 percent capacity. Neither does the body. Or the spirit. This, in itself, is not alarming. This humanness does not necessitate a doctor's diagnosis.

Point: Some, perhaps many, aches and pains of the mind, body, and soul are simply evidence of the human condition. The bumps in our daily road through life remind us constantly that life is not easy. Nobody is constantly perfect and happy.

Take this test: Next time you drive past a school, count any 24 children on a playground. Two will become insane, four profoundly neurotic, four deeply neurotic, four mildly neurotic. Just 10 will grow up as fairly normal.

Some mental illness has been proven to be genetic but most are not. And the good news: most are curable. The cure lies in changed behavior, with the aid of professionals, and at the heart of the change is a sense of good feeling about self. Family and environment are important ingredients in the identification and treatment of people problems, whatever their degree of severity.

Most people develop problems because they are unable to cope with or adapt to the stresses and strains of everyday living at home, work, or play. Many people have what are called nervous breakdowns. Nerves, in fact, do not break down. The body does. Life force does.

People turn stress and problems into ulcers, headaches, and other chronic ailments. Research shows that cancer and heart disease can result from high levels of negative stress or poor self-concept. No, you don't get ulcers from what you eat; you get them from what's eating you.

Some pain can be avoided by facing problems and handling them — coping, making adjustments, and finding positive outcomes to negative events.

Most people with deep underlying problems are identifiable because they are reticent, shy, self-effacing. They put themselves down. A small percentage will strike out, sometimes violently — either at others, or at themselves — if provoked excessively, taunted cruelly, or repeatedly demeaned into humiliation.

Warning: treating people as objects deters them from developing self-esteem and self-respect.

Good news: treating people as people — with interest, understanding, compassion, education, and open, honest communication — gives them the opportunity to build self-confidence and increase their capacity for trust and responsible behavior toward themselves and others.

* * * * * * * * * * *

The worst sin toward our fellow creatures is not to hate them, but to be indifferent to them; that's the essence of inhumanity.

— *George Bernard Shaw*

* * * * * * * * * * *

An essential key to healthy living is self-respect and self-care. Learn to recognize and stave off what I like to call Nine Deadly Sins against yourself, ranging from feeling that nobody cares to the worst extreme (and waste) of all — suicidal tendencies.

Loneliness

Every last one of us feels lonely at one time or another. Loneliness is one of the most common human conditions. Feelings of isolation typically set in when you find no immediate replacement for an enjoyment of a past situation.

Most of that involves a personal relationship. Perhaps estrangement from one or both parents. Perhaps distancing of former friends who seemed to have turned their back on you. Or, as is often the case, perhaps separation from a significant other, a breaking up with a boyfriend, fiancé, or spouse.

The feeling also can stem from displacement from a job, or a move to a strange place where you know no one and find yourself sitting at home alone at night.

Probably the strangest and hardest state of loneliness to comprehend is that which exists even when none of the aforementioned conditions exist. The loneliness simply takes root at the core of your existence, stemming from a feeling of abandonment, even if only imagined.

When loneliness occurs, the most important antidote is to avoid abandoning yourself. It is a time to be good to yourself through whatever means you have learned through the years. Treat yourself to something nice — an event, new clothes, a good book. Seek out a friend or relative whom you trust and enjoy.

And a surefire way to stimulate happiness is to make someone else happy. Find and comfort somebody who is worse off than you.

Anger

You can find some books that say anger is a healthy emotion. Bunk. Anger too often rages out of control and results in destructive behavior, often violently. Anger grows powerfully, feeds off itself, and is contagious. Controlling anger is difficult, and requires strong understanding and self-discipline to control.

True enough, if anger is expressed (that is, released) properly and effectively, it can lead to positive change. Anger is energy, and must go somewhere. That is why in anger management counseling, the counselor will suggest such things as exercise (especially running), squeezing a ball, and even going to an isolated place and yelling (scream therapy) in order to release the energy of anger in a non-destructive way. It's called venting.

Knowing when, where, and how to vent is healthy; but that is not to be confused with thinking of anger itself as healthy. Quite the contrary. Many persons find it difficult to express anger; therefore it builds and builds until it explodes in harmful ways. Letting the anger free through direct and honest communication (maybe even a mild outburst — "I'm angry, dammit!") is desirable; yet we have somehow come to believe that such openness might jeopardize a relationship. A healthy disagreement can, in fact, strengthen ties between two or more persons.

Discovering how to make it healthy is the hard part. But if mounting anger is your typical reaction when you disagree, then seek counsel on how to express it, lest you storehouse it at a high cost to yourself and your important relationships.

Otherwise, many defensive actions are inevitable. Gossiping and back-biting are examples. Another is sabotage, by, for example, being constantly late. Communication becomes indirect, hostile, dishonest, and manipulative. And usually, when anger prevails — whether openly or simmering beneath the surface (then we call it different things — "I'm NOT angry, I'm just frustrated ... irritated ... aggravated …") — the real issue does not get dealt with.

Everybody is too busy just being angry, and either venting it in strong, disagreeable ways, or not at all. Watch out especially for the not at all.

Suggestion: find a really good book, such as "The Dance of Anger," (there are dozens on the library or book store shelves) and learn how anger comes from within, and therefore how you can learn to manage it in ways that are not self-destructive.

Depression

This is a wolf (anger) in sheep's clothing. And the wool you have pulled over your eyes is blue.

Depression ranges from that state of vague anxiety that we call the "blues" to the serious extreme of lack of interest in life.

Many specific situations can trigger depression. A common one, believe it or not, is a holiday, especially Christmas. Isn't that ironic? All the commercial gaiety and holiday cheer that is forced upon us can work to exaggerate feelings of being alone or anxiety about your core being. Or, the holiday can trigger memories of happier times when certain people were part of your celebration and now they are not — grandparents, a spouse, children who have grown up and moved away.

Other circumstances that at face value would appear to be high times, frequently lead to sinking spells. Perhaps you have read about mothers who become depressed after giving birth, or were depressed during the pregnancy because of the way they looked. Or, a soldier upon returning to civilian life.

And virtually all of us have experienced the depression of losing a close relative who died.

Whatever the cause or symptoms, never let depression go and grow unattended. You know how doctors say listen to your body? Well, listen to your soul, too. When it feels downtrodden and woeful, seek evaluation and professional help.

Typical statements that indicate depression:

"I feel downhearted."
"I'm blue."
"I'm bummed out."
"I can't sleep."
"I'm just not interested in anything."
"I feel like crying all the time."
"I don't want to get up in the morning."
"Sex? I couldn't care less."
"Nobody needs me any more."
"I'm so grumpy."
"I feel nothing. I feel numb."
"Sometimes I just wish I was dead."

Jealousy and Envy

All people confront jealousy at some time during the life cycle. You would be abnormal not to. It stems from moments of insecurity, to various degrees, when we fear that something of ours might be or has been taken away from us.

Most often jealousy is associated with a strained relationship in which one person appears to have lost affection for the other and has shifted it to someone else, real or imagined. Jealousy leads to counter-productive behavior such as possessiveness, distrust, "grilling" a partner on their whereabouts and the company they are keeping. The antidote is open and honest communication of your feelings so they can be either affirmed or disquieted.

Envy results from coveting something you want desperately that someone else has or gets — new possessions, a promotion, perceived status of some sort.

Goal: Learn to harness your needs and wants into attainable, realistic goals, separating them from things and situations that are totally inaccessible. That will eliminate jealousy and envy, which are usually petty and harmful to yourself and others.

Fear

One of the biggest demotivators known to man is fear — an emotion that is downright crippling, totally paralyzing a logical mind and functioning body.

Fear causes a person to retreat into him/herself and move away from society at large, and to resort to compulsive and ritualistic behavior to ward off danger. Or worse, it causes panic and loss of all control.

Certainly, we are confronted with real, frightening situations. Confrontation by an armed person in an isolated area comes to mind. Or, the feeling as you are being wheeled into surgery, which can be fear of the unknown, or fear of the serious nature of the condition.

But very often anxiety attacks set in when the cause is not known consciously. The recollection of a bad auto accident can subconsciously make a person afraid to get behind the wheel, where someone who doesn't know about it might think they are being irrational. There are instances where the mere thought of a dinner party gives the host or hostess a headache.

Some fears reside deep in the psyche. Why should a pregnant woman be fearful of bearing a son, or a reasonable man have a terrible phobia about tunnels or elevators?

Only by facing fear directly in the face on all levels can you learn to recognize and overcome the perceived dangers, whether real or imagined.

Keep in mind that bravado is not the answer to fear. The stiff upper lip is just another term for denial, and that does you no good whatsoever. A book title comes to mind as a good rule of thumb for most fearful situations: "Feel the Fear, and Do It Anyway." That is, of course, short of the extreme fear of bodily harm, where the best advice would be, "Feel the Fear, and Get the Heck Out of There."

In many situations that are far less dire, an easy exercise to help you overcome the fear is the Worst Case Scenario. Simply list the worst things that can result if you walk straight into the face of the fear; you'll be surprised at how often the worst thing is not fraught with terrible consequences.

Procrastination

Have you done this yet today, or are you putting it off?

Seriously, this is a killer word in a jungle of impotency. Who isn't plagued by it? And just when the battle appears to be won — inspired by a Time Management device or self-help book — it appears again.

One report suggested that the patent office registry in the U.S. would increase by millions if all inventive dreamers followed through on their ideas. Procrastination dwells among us all. Some more than others, of course — but it is a problem that behooves us to recognize and deal with, because it can be very costly, not only in terms of time and money, but in emotional and mental well-being.

Alcoholism

Statistics are endless and staggering. By the time teens reach the 12th grade, more than half will consume alcohol once a week. Nearly half of teenagers who admit to drinking say they have been drunk at least once.

The average amount of alcohol consumed by juveniles is increasing at alarming rates. Why not? After all, this Bud's for them. The advertising for alcoholic beverages is numbing.

Equal rights extend to drinking, too. Girls have caught up with boys in boozing. Problem drinking is devastating, at all ages, taking place in epidemic proportions. Most sociologists and experts in prevention and addiction treatment agree that alcohol is the "drug of choice" as the principal means of escape.

The number of young persons who die in drunk-driving accidents every year has reached six figures, and about half as many are disabled or disfigured. And most of these accidents are caused by young persons.

Solutions here are not easy. But easy isn't the issue. Somehow, we have to take the drink out of kids' hands, where, unbelievably, the problem starts before the teen years.

Stress and Tension

Medical experts have long believed that stress plays an important part in the development of ulcers. More recently, evidence is strong that unmanaged, negative stress is a symptom among other illness profiles — back problems, chronic headaches, other stomach ailments, and most drastically, heart disease and cancer.

Harried existence is at the heart of negative stress. Tension lingers long after a stressful event takes place. Tension is a revolt of unresolved inner conflict.

The key word here is inner. Two things are important to recognize:

- Conflict is simply a signal that somebody's needs are not being met.
- The person whose needs aren't being met owns the conflict. That means you.

Take charge of your stress, and you automatically reduce your tension. You will end the clash between impulses that demand action and the counter forces that inhibit spontaneous action. In other words, deal with it, rather than ignoring it in hopes that someone else will, or that it will go away on its own.

Practice this simple exercise, and when you learn its lesson, you will have taken the biggest step forward possible in handling stress:

1. Write at the top of a piece of paper, "Causes of My Stress."
2. List all the things you think cause you to have negative stress.
3. Now, strike out the word "Causes," and change the heading to read, "My Stressors."
4. Below the list write another heading, "The ONE Cause of My Stress."
5. Beneath it write the word, "Me."

Yes, you, the person in the mirror. The medical term for all external events and persons involved in stressful situations is stressors. They just are, and how you react/respond to their existence determines whether your stress levels will be positive or negative, high or low.

You, not they, will determine whether you feel achy or angry or anxious or afraid or whatever. That's where the term "response-ability" comes from — your ability to respond favorably to perceived negative stressors. Take something as simple as a red light when you are in a hurry. Why are you wigged out, and the person in the next car is calm, cool, and collected? It's the same red light, isn't it? So the red light doesn't cause the stress — either yours (negative) or the other driver's (positive, or none).

There are many readings that talk about how life is a

small percentage of what happens to you, and a large percentage of how you deal with what happens to you.

The goal is not to get rid of stress (indeed, some stress helps us strive to excel — the old adrenaline rush at the heart of peak performance); rather, the goal is to manage it. To recognize the stressors, take a deep breath, take appropriate thought and action, and negate the tension.

The alternative is frequent visits to the medicine cabinet. Or worse.

Remember: There is only one cause of negative stress. The person in the mirror.

Suicide

This is the most difficult subject I will deal with, and the hardest to put into words. Just recently, during the writing phase of this manuscript, I visited an acquaintance from our church in the hospital after her attempt at suicide, sharing pizza at her bedside.

A flood of bad memories came over me. This was an adult, but I had dealt with mere children who took their lives while I was principal of the alternative high school in my community. Nothing hurt worse than the emptiness created by those suicides.

An interesting facet of the study of suicide is that statistics are far-ranging. In one report I read that 28,000 take place in a year; another report said more than 100,000. That's because of an interesting phenomenon: suicide carries such a stigma of shame and guilt that many go unreported. Families will report the deaths as accidental, natural, or undetermined.

Experts say that suicide probably occurs three times more often than the reported figures, and that attempts are most likely 10 times more frequent than the reported deaths.

Suicide, obviously, is the most drastic alternative to

dealing with problems — whatever the problems might be. And that leads to another disturbing observation: the stigma of suicide keeps many people in denial about it — both the suicidal person, and any persons in a position to deal with them — such as educators, and especially, parents.

Thus, we tend to see right past some symptoms, or chalk them up to normal behavior ("oh, they're just going through a phase"). And I have a concern about the apathy regarding suicide. We get very emotional and excited when people involved in war lose their lives. I don't find the same widespread alarm over the suicide rate.

Many countries throughout the world report increasing suicide rates among adolescents, placing it high on the list of causes of death during the teenage-to-young adult years.

Clearly, the internal pressures of adolescence are greater than in any period of human development. And greater than in any other era. Since World War II, it's become increasingly difficult to be a teenager.

The victims in suicide extend far beyond the person who took his/her life. It is an enormously tragic event for survivors. Grief, guilt, and shame mushroom among relatives and close friends who lament the needless waste and unfulfilled promise.

And we all are burdened with the seemingly unanswerable question — why?

A breakdown of family structure and/or a hectic home life prevail in many suicide cases. Rejection by family and/or peers is common, feeding the feeling of loneliness and being unloved. Or worse, unlovable. And therefore, unwanted.

Self-destructive behaviors can stem from facing a world of tension, competitiveness, pressures, and demands that are too much to cope with.

Suicide clues are generally divided into three categories:

- verbal
- behavioral
- situational

Always tell somebody, anybody, if you have the slightest inkling that a person is considering or might consider suicide.

Become a "helper" to a person in dire need, who is reaching out. Encourage the person to talk about the problems and dilemmas that are going on in his/her life. Urge the troubled person to seek counseling help.

Never ignore or deny the person's expressed feelings. Whatever others say they feel is real to them, even if it seems irrational or wrong to you.

In almost every situation as a "helper," work from the understanding that the suicidal person is contemplating death of the whole self in order to get rid of just a part of the self that the person finds too painful, despicable, shameful, hateful, or raw to live with. Speak to the person on those terms — with the goal of having him/her see that it's only a portion of self he/she wants to get rid of, not the whole self.

Appendix IV

People Are People: Part C

In conclusion, let's finish on an up beat. This ending might be titled, "What to Do, What to Do ." Or, to quote the famed poet e.e. cummings (who wrote everything without capitalization):

"yes is a world. and in the world of yes reside all worlds."

Yes connotes optimism. Yes promotes hope. Yes demands positive action. Can we do something about all the things we have discussed? Yes! Will we? Yes!

Here are some ways, and some affirmations to enlighten our paths:

"That day is lost on whoever has not laughed."

— *French proverb*

The human body can never sprout an ulcer, never be infected by anger, never be overpowered by nervous tension while laughing. It is physiologically and chemically impossible.

Learn to laugh. Force it, if you have to. We never stop laughing because we grow old. We grow old because we stop laughing.

* * * * * * * * * * *

With laughter as a good starting point, take responsibility for your own actions. Exercise your freedom to choose self-fulfilling behavior over self-defeating. Making any and every experience enjoyable and challenging is a choice.

Feeling good about yourself is a choice. Develop the habit of feeling good about yourself and your activities, and that helps eliminate any habit of becoming overly wrought when things go wrong.

You'll also discover that you are not alone. Life's struggles are pretty much the same for everyone. The good news is that you, we — each of us — can cope. With concerted, conscious choice and effort, you can improve your lot and make yourself happy.

Abe Lincoln once said in a speech, "Each of us is only as happy as we choose to be." And pursuit of happiness, remember, was so tantamount to our way of life in America that our founding fathers put it in the Constitution as an inalienable right.

Every human being thrives on power and control. So take control of your own mind, your own feelings, your own way of speaking to yourself and others, and your own behavior — and see how remarkably powerful you feel.

* * * * * * * * * * * *

Some things to recognize:

- As a unique individual, "sealed in" your body and mind, your natural tendency is to feel separate from others. This leads to thinking abut differences more than similarities.
- A person who has low self-regard and therefore lacks self-worth and self-love cannot feel comfortable with others, because he/she is not comfortable with the person in the mirror. That leads to avoidance and withdrawal, thus compounding the feeling of separation and isolation.

- Self-concept is at the heart of how you cope with problems. It will dictate your successes and failures. It affects every choice you make and everything you do. The implication is clear: think highly enough of yourself to treat yourself well.
- You cannot, must not, be pulled down to depths of low self-esteem based on what other people think or say about you. A gift to give yourself: the knowledge that just because somebody says something doesn't make it true.
- Another gift to give yourself: realize that most problems are larger in your mind than they are in reality. That does not mean to trivialize problems. It just means you are far more capable of resolving them than you sometimes feel.
- Everyone operates in two worlds — the real world (reality), and an illusionary world (fantasy). Reality is what you create. Whatever occurs is reality. Everything else is perceived. Some perceptions are perfectly valid; that's not the point. The point is that fantasy sometimes interferes with coping and solving problems because somehow the magic allows a person to avoid pain, escape anxiety, and not choose and create a satisfying reality.
- The greater the need to escape, the harder you cling to fantasy. If that seems harmless, know that it caps your potential for living a rich reality. Be a dreamer, and dream big, but you cannot subsist in a dream world. If you only daydream of a huge, marvelous, scrumptious cake, and you never mix and bake the cake, the result is starvation.

* * * * * * * * * *

Never apologize for choosing what will nurture you.

A Suggestion for Improving Self-Esteem

DO: Offer praise, approval, and affirmation whenever possible.

AVOID: Putdowns, sarcasm, name-calling, and harsh criticism.

(Footnote: This applies to yourself, as well as others. The practice of healthy self-talk is the most important communication that you will engage in.)

* * * * * * * * * * *

Life is like climbing a slippery hill. You climb, you slip, you climb, you slip. The test of success is, do you keep climbing, trying to get a little higher, or do you give up and quit climbing?

* * * * * * * * * * *

To Fuel Cheerfulness and Optimism:

- Learn as much as you can about yourself. Seek understanding about why you hold certain attitudes and biases. Keep only those that are useful and productive, and never let the others filter in to control your life.
- Be fully aware of your needs, yet avoid magnifying them out of proportion. Unfulfilled needs lead to frustration and anger.
- Talk about your problems with someone you trust to be a good listener. Otherwise, you will have a boiling cauldron in the pit of your stomach.
- Set realistic, achievable goals for yourself, based on your mission and values, not somebody else's expectations.
- Reject guilt over things that don't really matter.
- Increase your self-esteem. A reminder: esteem comes from Latin meaning "to value highly." Place high value on who you are, build yourself up.

- Change whatever makes you unhappy. Or at least change the way you think about it so you can be happy in spite of it.
- Take advantage of your body as an intricate machine with infinite coping skills and adaptive mechanisms. With a little introspection and effort you will realize alternatives and solutions to your crises. In other words, you can and will cope.

* * * * * * * * * * *

A Quick Mental Health Check-Up

1. Are you happy? Happiness is the first symptom of a good mental outlook.
2. Do you have a zest for life?
3. Are you socially well-adjusted? Do you enjoy being with other people?
4. Do you have unity and balance in your life?
5. Can you live with each problem as it arises?
6. Can you let go of the past, and stay worry-free about the future?
7. Do you have good insight into your own conduct?
8. Do you have a confidential relationship with another person?
9. Do you have a sense of the ridiculous? Can you laugh at yourself?
10. Are you engaged in satisfying work?

Examine every unsatisfactory answer for possible symptoms of depression or some other form of being off-center mentally.

Write a plan for moving toward a satisfactory position on all questions.

Seek counseling on some level (pastoral, professional, etc.) wherever it might help. Remember, counseling doesn't mean you are broken or weak or that something is bad or wrong with you; it simply means you need assistance from someone trained and skilled at helping you find solutions to problems.

* * * * * * * * * * *

Life is like chasing a butterfly. You can never quite catch one, but the moment you sit down and relax, the butterfly will come and sit on your shoulder.

* * * * * * * * * * *

Use the sample here to list assets and areas for improvement in seven key areas of your life. Use a sheet of paper for each area:

Mental
Physical
Career
Financial
Family
Social
Spiritual

First, assign each area a number, from 1 (very dissatisfied) to 10 (very satisfied), indicating how you feel about that area of your life at the moment.

That will give you an idea on where to start for achieving more balance, and which areas to give the strongest priority to. Now, list your assets in each area, the things you feel good about. Then, list your desired areas for improvement in each facet of your life.

Throughout the exercise, use the assets as affirmations about how good and worthwhile you are in many areas of your life. Plan ways to expand on the assets and practice them often.

With the areas for improvement, write an organized, specific, step-by-step program for making necessary changes to bring up your sense of well-being in each area of life.

This requires commitment and practice, direction and plans, dedication and perseverance.

With faith and some hard work you can move toward a bright new world of zestful living.

* * * * * * * * * *

Strengthening Communication Skills

One of the greatest gifts of humankind is the ability to speak and articulate with one another. We are not limited to mooing, bow-wowing, meowing, chirping, or whatever snakes do to talk.

In talking, we use language, with emphasis on words (or not), plus tone and volume of voice. Plus, we communicate through many channels besides talking. Body language speaks loudly. Eye contact. Arms crossed. Smile or frown. There is paralanguage (your clothing, the car you drive, the house you live in, your hair style, your perfume or after-shave, the books or magazines you read, TV or movies you watch — things outside of your language and body that speak volumes).

And a word about one other major, major ingredient in effective communication — listening. Communication implies a two-way interaction; for it to occur there must be a receiving station. If the words fall on unlistening ears, tied directly to a disinterested or preoccupied mind, then communication breaks down.

So the basics of productive communication are to speak honestly and clearly about what you need, want, or feel ... listen carefully when someone else does the same with you, whether that's in phatic communion (small talk!) or deep, serious discussion.

In effective communication, we find harmony, consistency, uniformity in the messages conveyed. We have a good sense of knowing what the other person is saying (and not saying), and where we stand with that person. We call it being on the same page, being in sync, in tune, or on the same wave length.

Breakdowns occur when messages are sent that are unclear, contradictory, ambivalent, confusing, and manipulative (the person is not saying what she/he really means). That leads to perplexity, anxiety, anger, and bad rather than desirable results.

Many myths get in the way, too. Sometimes people believe they can't communicate with people of dissimilar characteristics, e.g., adults who think they can't get through to children or teenagers (the age-old generation gap), racial barriers, gender barriers, social strata barriers.

There is no complex, secret, magical formula for communicating better with your children or parents, your teachers or bosses, your spouses or significant others, or people in general. The formula evolves heavily from common sense, rooted in the Golden Rule, and from want-to and practice.

You'll go far if you just speak to others as you would have them speak to you.

Some basic ingredients of effective communication include:

- Positive self-talk, rooted in self-esteem, which enhances positive talk to and about others.
- Empathy. Determine how you might feel if you were in

the other person's position or predicament, and how you might react.

- Lots of T.L.C. As you increase your capacity for caring, you will notice an improvement in your communication skills. The world is full of people who do not care about other people. Decline to join them.
- Accept people as they are. Avoid getting hung up on someone's appearance.
- Be fair. Nobody is perfect, everyone makes honest mistakes. Acceptance comes easier when you communicate that you know that, just like you, other people are doing the best they can with what they have to work with at that moment.
- Remain consistent. If you are up and down and all over the chart — pleasant this time I see you, unpleasant the next — chances are I will be leery of communicating with you.
- Honesty is at the core of good communication. Speak in a forthright manner, directly to the point, and never hedge or mince words on a difficult matter. This is not easy, but it can be done, and must be to earn and maintain respect and trust.

* * * * * * * * * * *

Finally, always keep in mind that the difference between a happy person and a broken soul is never problems. The difference is in a person's attitude toward problems. As the poet William Thackery put it,

Life is a mirror. If you frown at it, it frowns back; if you smile at it, it returns the greeting.

Keep smiling.

Charles Jackard has become one of the most sought-after keynote speakers and seminar leaders in the nation for educational, institutional, and public audiences. For more information on scheduling his appearances or to order copies of this book, please call or write:

Charles R. Jackard PMB #388
4318 Rainbow Blvd.
Kansas City, KS 66103

Telephone/Fax: (913) 648-7039

e-mail: snooper@qni.com